MW00997761

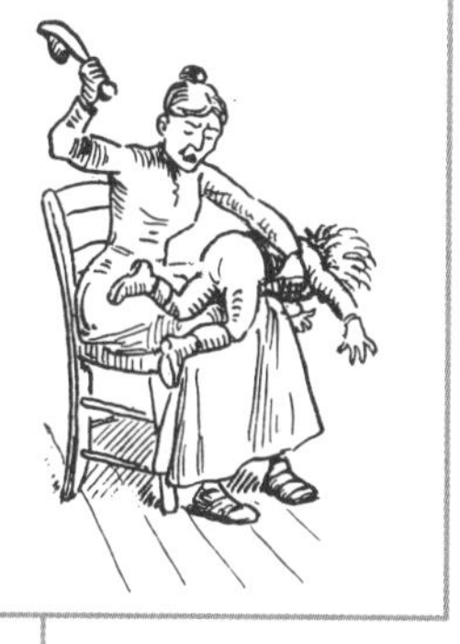

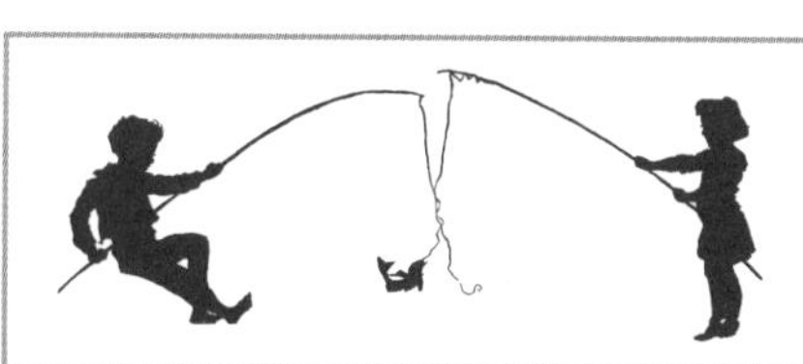

Ungovernable

Also by Therese Oneill

Unmentionable: The Victorian Lady's Guide to Sex, Marriage, and Manners

Also by Therese Oneill

Unmentionable: The Victorian Lady's Guide to Sex, Marriage, and Manners

Ungovernable

Ungovernable

The Victorian Parent's Guide to Raising Flawless Children

Therese Oneill

Little, Brown and Company
NEW YORK BOSTON LONDON

Little, Brown and Company
Hachette Book Group
1290 Avenue of the Americas, New York, NY 10104
littlebrown.com

First Edition: April 2019

Little, Brown and Company is a division of Hachette Book Group, Inc. The Little, Brown name and logo are trademarks of Hachette Book Group, Inc.

ISBN 978-0-316-48190-8
LCCN 2018958140

10 9 8 7 6 5 4 3 2 1

LSC-C

Book design by Fearn Cutler de Vicq
Printed in the United States of America

To the Two Mothers
to Whom I Owe Everyone I Love

Sandra Balmer Nagel
1943–2011

Gloria Schilling Smith
1924–2017

They were ***magnificent****, and they never would have done any of the things in this book.*

Contents

Author's Note

The Stuff of Nightmares

This book is full of true information about child-rearing in the nineteenth century. I describe real attitudes, real practices, real children. I have culled from that era what is strange, incredible, and darkly funny, particularly as it related to the upper class of both America and Britain.

This is handpicked history, not comprehensive.

The nineteenth century was, for many children, the most horrible time in history to be alive. Cities formed quick and dirty, and they were lawless, full of uncontrolled disease, crowding, exploitation, and abuse. People suffered tremendously as they tried to find their footing in a brutal new world. Children suffered worst of all.

There are many books that can educate you about that suffering. This isn't one of them.

I will address but not dwell on the misery of this era: the fact that during some periods of the nineteenth century, the child mortality rate was at 50 percent, or on the lack of child labor laws, or the fact that there was no such thing as "child abuse" until late in the century, when the ASPCA decided to incorporate children into their protection along with dogs and horses. I wrote *Ungovernable* to entertain and inform; I didn't write it to slug you in the stomach.

It is my dearest hope that the historically accurate pieces of child-rearing advice, history, and anecdotes I relate here will leave you stupefied and shocked. I hope the style I have set it in will be a thrill of an introduction and will allow you to pursue the topics deeper (and darker) if you desire. Thank you.

—Therese Oneill

Ungovernable

"We need to talk."

Welcome, Unfit Mother

So. Here is where your life choices have deposited you. Let's take a look, shall we?

Your bloodshot eyes and slouchy slept-in clothing. Your once-taut belly lapping over the yoga pants that will never come any closer to a yoga studio than the 7-Eleven it shares a parking lot with.

But here's some good news! You've finally found a way to make the baby sleep: you just have to keep one hand on her tummy while using your other hand to keep the wind-up baby swing swaying at precisely three-fourths time, and run the vacuum and dishwasher simultaneously, while making sure the spit-up-encrusted blanket she won't let you wash is tucked snugly around her left shoulder but never *touching* the right.

Now you are enjoying the first stillness of your day. You've made a little nest out of the least offensive dirty laundry that was clean yesterday before your older child overturned the basket from the sofa and used it to cage your middle child, who, defying six months of potty training, chose tactical targeted urination as an effective defense.

You went to rewash the towels but then both boys started throwing up, so the laundry that was merely peed upon had to take a back seat to that which had been puked on. The layer of plastic toys (the cheap, mass-produced cartoon abominations you swore you'd never buy) jab you through your makeshift bed, but the blessed side of total exhaustion is that you hardly feel them. Plus, ever since the last baby compensated for her slippery-quick birth by doing unspeakable things to your pelvic floor with her exit, you've accepted that pain is just part of life now. Let's lie back onto the intricately finger-painted yogurt stains that cover your couch, and *reflect*.

You wanted a baby. You wanted to love another human and shape them into a gift to give the world. Now, in your darkest hours, you fantasize about yourself before children, smugly popping each blue birth control pill out of its foil into your toilet. Had you access to a time machine, you believe you'd use it to push into that bathroom, rip the towel rack off the wall, and knock your idiot self into the tub. Then you'd fish every last pill out of the bowl. It doesn't matter if they've dissolved...back then you kept the toilet clean! The powder will dry and you can mix it with the *expensive* yogurt you used to buy, in the Before Time.

And here you are. Huddled in garbage, chained like a low-rent Princess Leia to a pumpkin-sized Jabba the Hut, fantasizing about time machines and toilet pills. Aw, honey. It's okay. This is a confusing time in your life.

You're a twenty-first-century parent living in a world where the rules of proper parenting change by the hour. And you're starting to think...they're *stupid* rules. Stupid and useless, and they've crushed your faith in any writer with letters after her name. Still, you're desperate. You keep hoping to grab ahold of a book with the *right* set of rules.

Judging by the way your chipped manicure scrabbled over the

"This Is What I Call a Monster!"
by E. A. Oneill, age ten, 2017.

spines in the childcare section of the bookstore before settling on this peculiar book, you've still not found the magic words that will transform your sloppy, non-subservient progeny into something you can show off in public. In fact, you're beginning to despair that you ever will. That you have done, and are continuing to do, everything wrong.

Oh, you poor woman. Pause. Breathe. And accept the truth.

You *are* doing everything wrong. You're a mess and your parenting is woefully lacking in nearly every regard.

I'm not telling you this to be harsh. Truly, I'm here to help, but we can't begin the healing process until you face the mess you've gotten yourself into. The proof is all around you. And not just in the abhorrent behavior of your children.

Look at what a fibber you've become! You know "screen time" is bad...so you find yourself saying ridiculous things like, "My children watch two hours a week and they only like 1970s-era *Dr. Who* episodes that we get on VHS from the library! Or for a special treat they can watch YouTube videos of DR Ramasjang. It's Danish children's programming notable for its open acceptance of cross-dressing puppets." But that's not counting the days when you're tired, busy, or out of wine. Which is every day now. Then you strap them down in front of whatever screen in the house blinks brightest and loudest.

Or the lengths you've gone to conceal that your child only eats four foods. And they're all brown, except for that purple cereal you buy direct from Amazon so no one will see your shame. And you never thought to feel bad about the half swat on the rear you gave your son when you found him atop the family Pekingese, squeezing the contents of an entire honey bear over her $120-per-groomer-visit coat, but now you press your hands to your guilty brow, wondering if you're a child-beater. (You're not, by the way. However, butt-swatting is an ineffective punishment. Unless you're using properly aged and cured hickory switches.)

Then you compound your misery by seeking the most modern, educated advice you can find. Modernity has *nothing* to do with children, Mater. Children are ancient and unchanged in their pure form. You won't be helped by books that detail the importance of neutral color tones and non-judgmental chair design in your child's time-out space, or books that tell you never to call your daughter pretty but to encourage her when she elbows the old lady blocking her access to the frozen vegan pizzas at the grocery store, because she is showing leadership skills.

And where is the book that can explain how you're supposed to feel about the selection of satin demi-cup padded training bras next to the Dora the Explorer underpants? That feeling of disgust quickly shoved down by shame was so confusing, wasn't it? After all, you're supposed to...encourage a young woman's body acceptance and allow her to feel comfortable in her budding sexuality...right? But does that mean your eleven-year-old gets fancier bras than you? Does that seem fair to you?

Has it ever, in history, been so acceptable for a parent to be whipped by her child, instead of the other way around? Are you really surprised these methods aren't working?

Allow me to reframe.

Once upon a time, parents were not enslaved to the whims of ultra-confident toddlers. Once upon a time, you told a child to pick up his plate after he'd eaten *everything* you'd placed on it, and to put it in the sink. You told him one time. *One.* You did not count to three. You did not lob half-hearted threats regarding loss of iPad privileges. You simply told him to act and he did, respectfully. Dickens's Tiny Tim would have wept with gratitude over your heart-smart lentil loaf, not whined and gagged throughout the meal.

Once upon a time, if your daughter was taking too long gazing at her reflection in the mirror, you'd ask her to quote three verses from the Bible on vanity. And she would, from memory, effortlessly but with proper humility, and then quietly set aside her hairbrush and ribbons, ready to do whatever task you'd prepared her for. Did Beth March simper and flounce when she was unable to attend the ball her older sisters were taken to? No! She died with quiet dignity!

Once upon a time your fourteen-year-old son would hold a broken vase in front of you and look truly shamefaced. And when you said, "Clean this up, and we'll talk about this when Father gets home. Now go help the men in the barn," he would exit the room in stricken silence. Would the boy smartly suggest a better place for you to keep your vase so as to avoid poor fellows accidentally bumping into it? Would he scream that you don't understand him and never take his side? Would he say, "You're a total WAD, Mother!" and slam the door on his way out to the bicycle *you* bought for him to pedal himself to the arms of some purple-lipstick-wearing eighth-grade harlot? *No.* Even Huckleberry Finn, with all his adolescent mischief, took his drunken

"The happy mother. Not you."

father's constant beatings in easy stride. Young boys had resilience back then. Set them atop a raft made of garbage and send them down the Mississippi River—yes, they might encounter some floating corpses and a handful of attempts on their lives, but they didn't *fuss* about it. They were too busy building character.

There was once a time when parents *were gods,* and children their humbled flagellants! Good times! And, my friend, we can bring those days *back.*

Imagine that you had the chance to consult with the sage experts whose advice (probably) shaped the maternal minds that produced Thomas Edison, Winston Churchill, Florence Nightingale, and Lord Baden-Powell. (He founded Scouting for children. Without him there would be no Eagle Scouts. Eleven of the twelve men to walk on the moon were Eagle Scouts. Thus, without Lord Baden-Powell, America would not own the moon. No, we do. Law of Finders, Keepers.)

Would you do it? Or would you stick to more modern childcare books, with their unrealistically upbeat insistence that a child is a person, one deserving respect and consideration? Or, worse, the books written that helped create *your* insufferable generation? (Perhaps you should ask your husb—excuse me, co-parent partner to set down the game controller he's currently using to massacre aliens while arguing via headset with a twelve-year-old in New Zealand about who "boinked" whose mom first to weigh in on the matter?)

A child is like a large insentient rock. Just a large, heavy burden with no obvious use. A parent is a stonemason. This child could be so hauled, smashed, and chipped away at that he is fit to form the supports of Halls of Governments, Grand Cathedrals, or An Especially Nice Applebee's in the Good Part of Town. Or, if you continue on your course of twenty-first-century child-rearing, he could become that misshapen boulder that hangs over the railway bridge on River Road, the one where all the seniors at the high school paint penises in their class colors.

In this book I have anticipated your questions and compiled all the very best parenting advice from nineteenth-century experts. Here you will learn about discipline, morals, and the devastating repercussions of allowing a child to eat fruit. Set yourself free from the agonizing politics and pressures of twenty-first-century parenting. They aren't working anyway. It's time to take children back to the old school.

1

How Do I Prepare My Sacred Vestibule to Best Receive My Husband's Life-Germ?

The Ins and Outs of Fruitful Conception

Try to assume as close to a left-bend forty-five-degree angle as possible to shorten the male-gender ovum's journey through the fallopian tubes.

Q: Do you have any advice if I'm still on the fence about having children?

A: Yes. Every moment you remain childless is another beat of your heart echoing down a meaningless eternity. Your time on earth will have been a blip, a glitch, and no trace of you will escape the blankness of death, and when you are gone only the poor estate agent who has to try to rid your home of your stench will mourn your passing.

Q: Oh. Well. That's a pretty tight argument. Except I have child-free friends who are doing just fine.

A: Child-*less* is the proper Victorian term. Actually, "barren" is more accurate. "The Lord hath turned His mercy against you" is also appropriate. Your childless friends *seem* happy, with their disposable income and spare time. But how they weep at night. Weep in their clean houses after eating expensive adult food and wine and watching rated-R movies on the big screen in the living room. *Bitterly weep.*

But this is moot! You already know, in your heart, that children are your highest purpose as a woman! Otherwise you'd never have picked up this book. Let's get started! Your work as a good mother begins long before the birth of your precious children. It begins even before conception! Preparation for motherhood as the Victorians did begins the moment you awkwardly allow your new husband to bunch your thirteen pounds of nightdress around your waist and accidentally elbow you in the chin while blindly but earnestly trying to navigate the cartography of your lady parts. If things get weird, just remember, you're doing this for the baby!

Q: Wait—do I have to wear the nightdress? Weird how? What sorts of things am I supposed to do to prepare?

A: Slow down there, feisty filly. I don't mean to mislead you. While it is the highest and most noble desire to start a family, it's not a privilege to be allotted to *all* women. First, you must ask yourself, "Is it a good idea to put more of *me* in the world? Would my offspring bring good to society, or would I just be mushing up all my own deficiencies, from my foul temper to my freckles, into a squalling eight-pound plague to unleash on civilization?" Now is not a time to mince words, so I must say with great solemnity: We don't more need more stupid and ugly in this world. If inferior goods are all that's on offer up your baby aisle, best to just convert it into a dry goods department.

Dr. L. C. Winsor wrote an editorial in an 1887 edition of the *Obstetric Gazette* called "Should Conception Be Controlled?" about stupid people making new stupid people. Lack of sense and restraint was, in the doctor's opinion, killing America.

> *It cannot be disputed that the majority of our race are conceived utterly regardless of the conditions, time, or of the fitness of the parents to procreate. Such being the case, is it strange that we hear now and then rumors that the American race is becoming weak? That hollow chested, round-shouldered, debilitated fathers, and worn, dyspeptic mothers, complain that the children are sick so much that they are turning home into a hospital?*

And what is to blame for this degradation of the American

breed? Says Winsor, "Men and women are too prone to marry on simply the one quality—that of love."

There it is. Mushy, squishy, imprudent "love." Ruining humanity by not factoring sensible breeding into the equation. Winsor continues:

> *Often the fitness as regards health, temperament and inclination are totally disregarded. Few men are as strong as their ancestors were. They are not of the rugged puritan type, nor is the tendency in America to strength, but rather to weakness, and under these circumstances, with no especial preparation, conception takes place.*

Q: Wait—"rugged puritan type"? Didn't half the *Mayflower* Puritans die, precisely because they were too weak to survive freezing, sickness, and starvation, all within months of landing in America?

A: Ha! No! That's just...I mean...like *barely* half! There were 102 *Mayflower* passengers and only 45 or so died by the first winter. Besides, the good doctor obviously isn't referring to the ol' "Oh, poor me, I can't survive an unusually harsh New England winter in a badly built shelter with hardly any food and now I'm going to die because I haven't the fortitude to walk off a little bit of scurvy" Puritans. He's talking about the hardy survivors that built America! And look: An Object Lesson. Bring weak humans into the world, force the Lord to cull them out.

How cruel of you.

This is why you must be sure you're worthy of procreation. Do not be one of the "thousands of careless, selfish and vicious couples" identified by Lyman Beecher Sperry in 1900's *Husband and Wife* who are unfit to marry but do it anyway. You must self-

"No, I'm really happy to be in the New World. It's just I only brought this one cape and I don't know how to make houses happen."

govern. Because modern minds apparently consider it a "gross violation of human rights" to implement Sperry's suggested solution: "Of course, it would be great gain if all those who ought not to reproduce their kind could be prevented from marrying; but at the present stage of human development such a method of preventing the multiplication of defectives is too radical to secure favorable consideration."

Q: "Preventing the multiplication of defectives"...wasn't that one of Hitler's programs?

A: I'm very eager to answer all your questions, but we'd move faster if they weren't all directed at poking holes in my historical narrative. Furthermore, if you attach Hitler's name to *anything* it's going to sound over the top. Granted, forced sterilization is already...rather fringe. And, yes, the Nazi Party enacted many laws to prevent the birth of "unsound progeny" by sterilizing people who were judged by an investigating panel as unfit...but... the Victorian eugenicists didn't mean to be *evil.* Victorians lived in a largely speculative world, full of ideas on how to improve their changing civilization. They weren't great at factoring in the wild variable that is human behavior. Since they intended good, they wouldn't easily conceptualize just how awful such a method would be when put into action. It doesn't change the fact that you *yourself* have a moral duty to find out if you're fit for reproduction.

Q: And how will I know if I am fit for reproduction?

A: Science will tell you! Victorian science, which is a little different from what you're used to, since it's not big on evidence or whatever. It was a system based more on...intuition! Of men! Who may or may not be scientists but who *do* love to write books with big, big words! So, listen.

Obviously you should not reproduce if you are cursed with any sort of illness that might be passed on to your offspring or impair your ability to care for them. Neither should you reproduce if your IQ is below average, but that's rather moot. As Sperry tells us, dumb people are always the last to know of their condition. Nonetheless, let's look at some of the ladies who are fouling the gene pool and need to be banned from the "recreation" center.

Girls Under Twenty Years of Age—*The Physical Life of Woman: Advice to the Maiden, Wife, and Mother* by George Henry Napheys was reprinted decades past its original 1869 publication, so popular was his advice regarding the weaker sex. Even though early marriage was far more acceptable in the past than today, Napheys recognized that a woman under twenty is rarely physically or mentally prepared for the demands of motherhood. Plus, she's probably going to die: "It is very common for those who marry young to die young. From statistics which have been carefully compiled

Tight-lacing the corset of a twelve-year-old gives the appearance of fuller hips and breasts, but that is usually only an illusion brought on by organ displacement.

[he doesn't have those statistics *on* him at this exact moment, but trust him, they were wayyyy carefully compiled], it is proven that the first labors of very young mothers are much more painful, tedious, and dangerous to life, than others." If young mothers don't die right away, Napheys warns, they will certainly suffer barren wombs. Or, unpredictable little tarts that they are, go completely the other way and live a long time and have way too *many* children. Seriously, anything could happen! Almost to the point that it seems totally random and not worth medical notation. Although you can be sure the children of a young mother are predestined to be societal burdens.

Death deals a mercy blow to an industrious wife before her feverish work ethic can weaken the human gene pool.

> *The children of [young] marriages are rarely healthy. They are feeble, sickly, undersized, often with some fault of mind or body, which is a cross to them and their parents all their lives. They inherit more readily the defects of their ancestors, and, as a rule, die at earlier years than the progeny of better-timed unions.*

But don't wait too long, either.

Elderly Women Over Thirty Years of Age—If you have been regularly shucking out fine little corn nubbins throughout your twenties and into your later years, never fear: Napheys approves of your output. But if you are one of those unfortunate spinsters planning to conceive for the first time past your sell-by date, beware. Of course, the decision is up to you, but keep in mind that you're probably going to die. Says Napheys: "The first labors of wives over thirty are nearly *twice* as fatal as those between twenty and twenty-five."

Industrious Women—It was a conundrum, as Americans settled the West in the mid-1800s, how such fierce pioneer women—women who survived wars, disease, and privations—could in turn birth a generation of girls who lounged on fainting couches sipping cordials to treat their migraines. Dr. John D. West related the lamentation of one such strong woman in the 1886 edition of *Maidenhood and Motherhood, or Ten Phases of a Woman's Life:* "Why is it that my daughters have no powers of endurance? Why, the three girls together cannot do the work I could when I was their age. Why, what would have become of us if I had been lying around in silk wrappers and satin slippers, dosing with drugs, as my girls do?"

The answer, fierce yet foolish woman, is that there was only *so much* vitality to go around during your pregnancy, and you hogged it all. You decided it was more important to build cabins and dig wells than to sit quietly, calmly incubating your young charge. Your blind greed for water and shelter sapped the fortitude of your fetus. Says Dr. West, "The poor old woman...robbed them [her children] of their inheritance by using all her vitality in her daily avocations, and they must suffer for her wrong-doing."

Belgians. The Silent Scourge.

Belgians and Other Poor People—According to Dr. West the Belgian people are an excellent example of the scientific fact that "the number of children born is in inverse proportion to the amount of food in a country and in a season. In Belgium the higher the price of bread, the greater the number of children, and the greater the number of infant deaths."

Well, Belgium? Have anything to say for yourself?

Q: So...when is my body most fertile?

A: You know how you're always supposed to handle a gun as if it's loaded, even if you're certain it isn't? Same goes for your husband's penis.

So even though Dr. Napheys advises couples who wish to postpone parenthood to marry on a day halfway through the bride's menstrual cycle, since this time is her "season of sterility," it's best to assume that gun is still loaded.

Q: Especially since my ovulation test says that's just about the *most* fertile time in my cycle.

A: If you're going to use things like ovulation charts and home pregnancy tests and science, you might as well abandon this whole Victorian endeavor. Are you in this or not? You want the baby given to you by a merciful God and abundant nature, or do you want a chemical pee-stick baby?

Q: A what?

A: Besides, those newfangled ovulation charts don't even factor gender into their calculation. As Dr. West states with firm assuredness, "It is now pretty conclusively established, by the most reliable scientific tests, that males or females can be produced at will." And if you want the secrets to success (a boy), you have to get it from the wisdom of ages past.

Dr. West is referring to a popular theory of the day often called Thury's Law, which proposed that gender relied on the *ripeness* of the female egg. Therefore, as laid out in *Husband and Wife,* by Sperry:

"1. Those who desire a female child should endeavor to secure impregnation as soon after menstruation as possible, hoping that the ovum may not yet be too ripe to produce the sex desired.

2. Those who desire a male child should defer impregnation until from about seven to eleven days after the cessation of the menstrual flow, hoping that by that time the ovum may be sufficiently ripe to produce a male child."

"I really value our chats about my menses, Jed."

Q: I'm not sure that theory deserves the descriptor "Law." Maybe "Thury's Got This Far-Out Idea—Dude, You Gotta Hear This"?

A: Yes. It's natural to mock what we don't understand. But you should know, West isn't the only subscriber to Thury's *Law.* West cites a carnival of experts, including "a farmer in Louisiana" who wrote a similar theory of reproduction in the periodical *Turf, Field and Farm.* The farmer said, using Thury's Law, "I have already been able, in many cases, to guess with certainty the sex of a future infant. More than thirty times, among my friends, I have predicted the sex of a child before its birth, and the event proved nearly every time that I was correct." No, farmers are not doctors. They're *better.* They don't just grow humans—they grow everything from okra to hound dogs! Who else would a sensible woman want advice from on the subject of breeding? And this particular farmer, he must have been absolutely outstanding in his field to engender these sorts of confidences from so many women.

Q: That's just flat-out wrong. On so many levels. But at the very

least, it's the Y chromosome in the sperm cell that determines gender.

A: How do you know that? Honestly, what is this "chromosome" people like to talk about so much? Have you ever seen one? Held one in your hand? Or do you just believe they exist because everyone says they do? Don't be such a sheep, woman. Gather all the information before you make a decision. If Thury's Law isn't good enough for you, try one of the gender-determining methods laid out in Thomas Washington Shannon's *Nature's Secrets Revealed,* first published in 1904: "Terry's Theory.—Terry gives as a tested and proved theory that if the wife is in a higher state of sexual vigor and excitement at the time of conception, boys will be conceived; but if the reverse is true, girls will be the result."

Dr. Stockham's Idea—Alice B. Stockham, M.D., believes that sex is in the soul. In that case, the sex of the offspring must be determined by a law of the soul. The parent whose mental forces previous to and at the time of conception are most active and vigorous controls the sex of the child.

Dr. Fowler's Observation—Dr. Fowler says that the greater male power and passion creates boys; female, girls. Conception right after menstruation gives girls, because the female is the most impassioned; later, boys, because her wanting sexual warmth leaves him the most vigorous.

So, to be safe, if you are desiring a firstborn son (which of course you are), you'd simply need to get yourself highly aroused while allowing your brain to go slack, to prevent your soul from impressing its femininity on your zygote. You'll also need to make sure your husband's brain is active *and* impassioned during the act… perhaps memorizing a few sexy calculus questions to pose during the most fevered moments of connection, precisely eleven days

"Train A, traveling at 70 miles per hour, leaves Intercourse, heading toward Climax, 260 miles away. At the same time, Train B, traveling at 60 miles per hour, leaves Climax, heading toward Intercourse. When do the two trains meet? Solve for se(x)."

after your period ends. Do all this and the odds are well in your favor that you'll conceive a son. Good odds. At least 51 percent.

Q: Are there other things I should do during the act of intercourse to encourage a fruitful conception?

A: Certainly. Venture to a warm climate, for instance, as Dr. West advises: "Climate and latitude have their influence upon fertility. More children are born to a woman in warm than in cold countries. This is owing very materially to the longer periods between the times of menstruation."

Dr. Napheys, referencing the great Hippocrates, reminds women to hold quite still post-coitus: "Sojourn on the bed after the act of generation," so that your husband's night deposit can be cashed in as quickly and smoothly as possible. To be safe, you

Alison uses an artificial breast pump to stimulate her uterus. Because her husband, Ronald, is the laziest man on earth.

should probably just remain immobile throughout intercourse. Well, you don't need me to tell you that. Any virtuous woman knows it's impolite to tussle.

Dr. West and Dr. Napheys both encourage a would-be mother to remember that breasts and womb are in direct connection. Therefore, stimulating one will affect the other. "There is a marked sympathy of the mammary glands and the uterus," says West; "hence, vigorous sucking of the breast before the generative act will, in many cases, insure conception." Prudes, take warning: "This is especially the case when barrenness is the result of coldness on the part of the wife."

Napheys, who is not nearly as fun as Dr. West, says nipple stimulation should be accomplished by borrowing someone's suckling baby (which seems a dreadful bait and switch to the poor little fellow) or using an artificial breast pump. Dr. Napheys should heed his Bible. God condones healthful loving foreplay. Just think of the Song of Solomon: "This thy stature is like to a palm tree, and thy breasts to clusters of grapes.... I will go up to the palm tree, I will take hold of the boughs thereof: now also thy breasts shall be as clusters of the vine." We will see in later chapters that perhaps not all of King Solomon's wisdom was beneficial for children, but this method was sound.

It is also important to be in a cheerful, mellow mood. Cranky sex makes cranky babies, says Napheys: "A being procreated at a period of ill humour, bodily indisposition, or nervous debility, may carry with it, during its whole existence, some small particles of these evils."

Be careful to not attempt procreation while in an ill humor. "You get home and start filling me with precious seeds of life right now, mister!"

The most important thing, however, is to be as sober as a stone when receiving your husband's life-germs. Intoxication is a subject that will recur many times in our discussions...many, many times. Frankly an awful lot more than you'd expect in a book devoted to childcare. And while drinking copious amounts of alcohol is never a wise thing to do when children are involved, even tangentially, the writers of Victorian baby-making advice were strict even by modern standards. Warns Napheys, "A condition of intoxication in the husband is a proper ground for refusal. Fecundation taking place while either parent has been in this state has produced idiots and epileptics."

Please do remember that in the nineteenth century, "idiot" was a legitimate medical term. Only later, in the twentieth century, would it be more likely applied to the sort of person who would say the things Napheys routinely said.

Q: What if I don't become pregnant right away? Does that mean I'm barren for life?

A: Oh, don't despair, my fruitless vine! There are myriad reasons for temporary barrenness that can be overcome. The first thing we must do is closely examine the flaws in your soul and work from there. Shannon cuts to the chase: are you a "Goodtime Gal"? Do you hang around ice cream parlors and vaudeville palaces and drink tea excessively? If so, you can expect plenty of male attention, but you secretly repulse them.

> *No man, influenced by pure love, can be attracted to a woman, as a husband, who lives on artificial excitements. All such, whether men or women, become impure, ugly and necessarily repulsive to true love. The sexual elements in all such become diseased, utterly corrupt and debased, and totally unfitted for the sacred function of reproduction.*

Known causes of sterility include endometriosis, chronic illness, and unwitting ballroom dancing with Satan.

Then again, you don't want to go too far in the other direction. Sperry raises the point that even a decent woman can spoil her reproductive organs through being a grumplepants: "Anxiety, fear, grief, suspicion, jealousy, anger, revenge, etc., are, for unknown reasons, strikingly preventive not only of conception, but also of normal ovulation."

So…stop being sad. Right now! "Feelings" are for artists and madmen. Sadness, fear, anger, are all emotions that can turn the body fluids that are supposed to welcome conception into vile baby-shunning serums. Sperry helps us understand.

> *Alarming and depressing emotions or intense excitement often*

> *cause such changes in the mother's milk as to render it actually poisonous to her nursing babe. Knowing these and kindred facts, we do not wonder that mental and nervous states can render male reproductive germs incapable of impregnating, and female germs incapable of receiving fertilization.*

West agrees. No baby wants to attain life inside a whiner's womb: "A frequent cause of barrenness and matrimonial unhappiness is a coldness and want of congeniality in temperament."

Q: Isn't there a possibility that my husband's biology might be contributing to our struggles to conceive?

A: Pshhh. I mean…it's not unheard of. But if your man *is* low on baby grain, you're not going to like the reason.

"The most common cause of impotency," Sperry tells us, "is sexual excess or abuse, resulting in collapse of the nervous mechanism of the reproductive system."

That means he's either spending all his good sperm on some other lady, or, more likely, in solitude. As in, he'd rather be masturbating in the dead of night behind the outhouse than sharing his glorious fecundity with you.

It may not be because you're abhorrent, however! Chin up! Maybe he's a Uranian, a condition we will learn of in later chapters. Or perhaps, without intending harm, you yourself are draining your husband of his vital fluids with your constant demands for carnal satisfaction. Men need time to re-seed. He's not a piece of meat, madam.

Dr. Michael Ryan points out that an overused seminal vesicle is a puny seminal vesicle. And that's no good; sperm must be sturdy and pistoned with great power toward its goal. Vaginas, especially gluttonous overused ones, are naturally inclined to

"Wilfred, what is the Matter?" Wilfred's "matter" is that you and your baby-starved seed-sucking womb need to back off for a bit.

deploy chemicals to fight invading germ-sperms. So a man's seed must have the force and guile to maneuver successfully through the shrewd labyrinth of your reproductive system.

"The most frequent cause of want of family, is too frequent intercourse," Dr. Ryan tells us. In such cases, "the male semen will be too weak, and the female will become relaxed, have increased mucous vaginal discharge, which will extinguish the vivifying principle of the male altogether.... All healthy persons who desire children, should cohabit but once or twice a week, and they will be seldom disappointed in their expectations. The sexual act is not performed well when repeated too often."

Q: Okay. Just...let's not talk about semen for a bit. Are there any other reasons for unsuccessful fruition that have been lost to history?

A: Mismating is seldom talked about today, though it was a serious consideration for most of the nineteenth century. So much that it was even considered in courts of law, as seen in Dr. Ryan's 1831 edition of *Manual of Medical Jurisprudence,* in which he warned that large and small people who tried to reproduce could expect difficulties, likely due to "the disproportion of the organs." "This is observed very often, when persons of extreme difference of stature cohabit," wise Ryan observed.

Throughout the century many men of learning believed that a

A prime example of a mismatched couple. Too many similarities, such as light curly hair and an unnatural passion for soup ladles.

husband and wife had to be of complementary physical and mental builds to successfully procreate. Napheys thought he had this one figured out. "The ancients and some modern authorities maintain that persons of the same temperament should not marry, as such marriage is likely to be unfruitful," he wrote. "Hence blonde women should marry dark men, thin women robust men, and vice versa. There is evidently a condition of sterility which is the result of mismating. The proof of this is seen where a woman remained barren in a first marriage but was fruitful in a second."

Q: Or maybe the first husband had fertility problems of his own—

A: Please! Will you mind your serpent tongue for a single *moment?* I think I've made it clear that suggesting a man is infertile in this era is akin to just flat out calling him a limp-membered chronic masturbator who must fantasize about being birched by his old schoolmaster to achieve climax. Sperry brings a little more science to the issue. For one thing, maybe it isn't your husband's fertile season.

Q: Oh. We're going to be talking about semen again, then.

A: You brought this on yourself. Sperry tells us, "In some instances the male produces spermatozoa and is fertile during certain periods of the year only. This seems to be natural with many species of inferior animals, and it probably explains the fact of the absence of any exhibition of sexual passion during protracted periods annually."

That is an incredibly reasonable correlation. Or causation. Fact! Reasonable probably-fact! Wait, he has some other very well-considered probably-facts. "Possibly nature has occult ways of knowing what is good or bad in such matters, and has also her secret methods of avoiding the one and securing the other." In other words, maybe Nature just *knows* that some people—say a gangly sallow redheaded anemic, for instance—have no business breeding with another of their kind, and refuses to take part in their propagation.

I'm not saying that's correct, of course. Some of my best friends are sallow redheads.

Q: Without modern tests, how shall I know when I am pregnant?

A: First of all, outside of this book, unless you're lecturing in a surgical theater to educated and properly emotionally stunted male doctors, don't use the word "pregnant." Just listen to it flop itself off the tongue. Ugh. "PRAYGNINT." It's a vulgar word, a gross shorthand of "I got a man's love squirts all up inside me and now my gut's churning up a bloody squish-baby for my vagina to squeeze out, so picture THAT, Aunt Lilah!"

You have any number of modest allusions at your disposal; use them. "With child," "expecting," "in the family way," and of course the French *"enceinte." Enceinte* has a multisource etymology, but primarily seems to refer to swelling beyond one's usual girding and becoming uncinched, or "uncorseted." Less appropriate but fashionable terms for pregnancies past include "to have sprained one's ankle," *"Hans en Kelder"* (Dutch for "Jack in the basement"…though it seems just as opaque in English without the Dutch), and "Here come the infantry."

Truthfully, Aunt Lilah already suspected as much.

Q: How shall I know when I have successfully sprained my ankle?

A: No, no, that's not how you use it. *Other* women whisper it about you behind your back! Ah, never mind.

If you're truly eschewing modern methods, confirming pregnancy will be a bit of a challenge. It wasn't until well into the twentieth century that scientists began to understand, much less measure, the hormone changes that conception caused in a woman's body.

That's when all the bunnies started to die.

Once she has conceived, a pregnant woman's placenta begins to produce a chemical called hCG, as well as elevated progesterone. By 1930 you could send off a sample of a woman's urine to a lab, where it would be injected into a sexually immature rat, mouse, or,

"Poor Jessica really needs to work on her balance. She seems to sprain her ankle just about every time she gets into bed."

most favorably, rabbit. If the animal began to ovulate, it meant it had been injected with hCG and the woman from whom the urine came was pregnant. Of course, you had to cut the rabbit open to check for ovulation. They didn't get sewn back up.

However, in the nineteenth century you would not yet know to look for answers inside the reproductive tracts of rabbit corpses. Pregnancy wasn't diagnosed easily, at least not officially. A woman might know quite well within herself that she was with child, but there was no way to conclusively convince anyone else.

Q: Why does she have to convince anyone else?

A: Courts of law took pregnancy very seriously. Whether or not a woman was pregnant at a certain time changed how certain legal issues were handled, from the execution of a last will and testament to plain old executions. A pregnant woman could not be hanged no matter what her crime.

A pregnant woman stands before a judge while an angry woman harangues a guilty-looking man.

For centuries, if a woman was sentenced to death, she could "plead the belly," claiming to be pregnant. This would stay her execution, and often resulted in her sentence getting buried in busy dockets and commuted to imprisonment. But proving she was pregnant was near impossible to do beyond a shadow of a doubt. Commonly, according to Alfred Swaine Taylor's 1853 edition of *Medical Jurisprudence,* a judge would commission a "jury of twelve married women" to determine if the woman was telling the truth. These women were "to be impaneled, and sworn to try, in the words of the law, 'whether the prisoner be with child of a quick child or not.' If they find her quick with child, she is respited; otherwise the sentence will take effect."

This method was only intended to determine a "quickened" child, meaning a fetus far enough into its development to have begun moving in the womb, usually the fourth or fifth month. Taylor recounts many cases where pregnant women were denounced as liars after their "medical" inspection, their lives (and their children's) only spared by a cautious judge holding the case in limbo for a few months to be sure.

Dr. Ryan's previously cited book on medical jurisprudence gives a frightening illustration of just how pitiful actual evidence for pregnancy was. For Ryan, the most reliable way to tell if a woman was pregnant was to observe her "moral state," which, in the case of pregnancy, "is subject to numerous changes": "Some women, naturally gay and amiable, become sad, melancholy, and insociable, and vice versa. Many diseases appear, others disappear, as hysteria, chlorosis, chorea, epilepsy. If all are present they afford strong proof of pregnancy, but never that positive certainty which enables us to give decisive evidence before magistrates."

Basically, you can tell she's pregnant if she seems...y'know...off.

At least Ryan knew enough to be dissatisfied with his method. And so, in the later nineteenth century, medicine and law began to work together to find ways to determine if a woman was faking a pregnancy. Still, no symptom by itself was solid proof of anything. Including these:

- **Ceasing to be "unwell"**—To stop getting your period seems the most obvious indication of pregnancy. But one of the reasons a modern woman's period is so darn periodical is that she is healthy, far healthier than her great-grandmothers were. Poor nutrition, arduous labor, the common occurrence of very early-term miscarriages that the woman was unaware of, and the continuance of spotting even when pregnant all contributed to the unreliability of this marker.

A nineteenth-century obstetric stethoscope, one of the few medical tools that were available and…all but useless in diagnosing pregnancy.

- **Swelling and discoloring of the breasts**—When a woman is pregnant, her breasts grow large to prepare for nursing and the areola darkens. Of course, noticing this requires having intimate knowledge of a woman's breasts beforehand, and is still subjective.
- **Morning sickness**—Vomiting and retching, usually lasting until "quickening occurs." Again, easily faked or caused by any number of nineteenth-century illnesses.
- **Detection of fetal heartbeat or movement**—Doctors often simply held an ear to a woman's stomach, or used very rudimentary stethoscopes, both inconclusive methods. Could be gas.
- **A growth in the abdomen**—Where at this point most of us would surrender and declare the woman pregnant, tumors and cysts in the female reproductive tract were often cited as the cause.
- **Pushing a small human out of her body**—Provided you can prove it's not a doll or monkey in a costume that was placed between her legs to look as if it emerged seconds before you saw it, this might serve as legal proof of pregnancy.

- Conversely, when *nothing* is solid proof, *everything* can be proof. Because it was an even more serious crime to conceal a pregnancy than to fake one. Hiding a pregnancy was considered criminal because it presupposed the grim question "What were you planning to do when you could no longer hide it?" Courts did not believe the majority of unwanted pregnancies ended with a baby warmly wrapped in a basket on the steps of a church.

Dr. Sperry tackles the less noticeable but just as likely secondary symptoms that afflict a pregnant woman. They include...ehh... every possible condition, illness, or irritation known to humans and most land mammals.

- The skin is apt to undergo decided alterations of appearance and behavior.
- Those who usually perspire freely are likely to have a dry skin during pregnancy, while those who usually have a dry skin may perspire freely...the perspiration in such cases is likely to have a decided odor.
- Women who are naturally pale before conception are apt to be florid during pregnancy, and those who are usually dark are quite prone to appear bleached, at least in spots.
- The lower lip is apt to protrude more than usual and the space below the eyes is frequently dark with venous blood. Troublesome skin diseases may appear at this time.
- A persistent loss of appetite and dyspeptic symptoms are not uncommon.
- Heartburn and flatulence are frequent.

- Marked drowsiness may result, and palpitations of the heart may give rise to unnecessary fears.
- The disturbed circulation and digestion are apt to produce constipation, or perhaps diarrhea instead.

Q: Sex calculus, sperm hoarding, breast-suckers, Belgians. Wow. I sort of just want a cat now.

A: Coward. Don't be intimidated! You're simply realizing the weight of your decision. Which, by the way, isn't really a decision. If you're a functioning, decent woman, motherhood is your duty to your civilization, your husband, and your God.

Dr. West can scold you better than I can. "Self and self-gratification is not the end of life. The peopling of the earth and the perpetuation of the race are ends residing in and proceeding from the marriage relation. It is the way instituted by the great Lawgiver for properly, wisely and safely consummating His purpose concerning the earth and man."

Or even more simply, here's a quote from the prolific nineteenth-century Scottish novelist Margaret Oliphant: "A house without a child is like a lawn without a flower."

Q: Is that really bad, though? Lawn without a flower? I try to keep my lawn completely green. The flowers I *do* get are dandelions and I'm constantly trying to kill off those little bast—

A: It's bad. *Empty,* she means. Devoid of color and vibrancy.

Bottom line: It's an abomination not to have children. Unless you're unhealthy, unpleasant, or unattractive—then it's an abomination to have them. But we're going to assume you belong to the former blessed band of breeders. So do as God commanded. And if divine wrath isn't enough to motivate you, Dr. West does make a good argument for the effort expended. Children may "bring care and trouble into the home"; they may "disturb its harmony, break up its quiet, scatter to the winds many of its carefully-observed rules. But," says West, "they bring more than they destroy. They teach patience, forbearance, kindness, sobriety, diligence, veracity, and all the nobler virtues of human life and character. They are the light and joy, the happiness and bliss, the virtue and peace, of marital life."

Like you were gonna retire young and backpack through Europe anyway. Many of us suffer lack of motivation to improve ourselves without being forced to. Kids are that force. Those little weeds may be the best thing that ever happens to you.

Although, as we will see, their germination isn't terribly fun.

2

How Much Violence and Lager Should My Fetus Be Exposed to as a Means to Ensure Sturdy Character?

And Other Pregnancy Tips

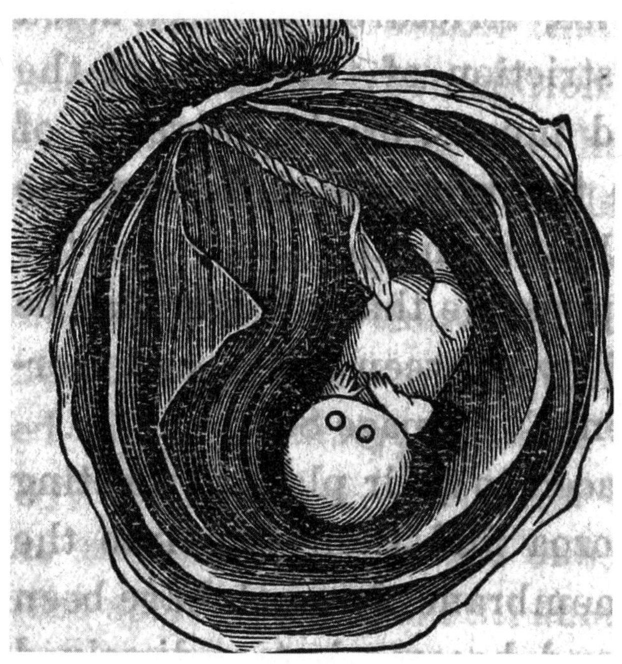

Congratulations. You got an A++ on the pee-stick test, or a gaggle of fishwives has stripped you naked and poked your belly to sufficiently convince the community you're not trying to deceive your way out of execution. Either way, you're pregnant.

If you approach this as a twenty-first-century woman, you'll want to immediately set to work ensuring the next nine months are healthy ones for both you and your growing baby. Throw out the allergy-causing peanut butter, nitrate-pumped prosciutto, mercury-tainted tuna fish, and all your favorite soft cheeses, because they weren't allowed to sit in a dark room long enough to grow a good thick mold that somehow fortifies against listeria.

Find the highest-quality prenatal yoga video you can stream. You can determine the best one by how expensive the New York loft it was filmed in looks. If you can't see exposed ductwork, it's not quality yoga.

Then up and down the aisle at the all-natural pharmacy you go, grabbing shea butter for your nipples and stretch marks, and vitamins the size of Christmas lights because folic acid...something something...bones? Doesn't matter—you just know it's absolutely necessary to your growing child. Don't forget the all-natural Jamaican ginger ale to ease your soon-to-come morning sickness. It's not going to help the puking but it *will* ensure you will never, ever be able to stand the taste of that particular soda again.

But then what? How frustrating it is, sitting home in your nest of prenatal commercialism with your still-flat belly, to have nothing to do but wait and worry.

How much more exciting for the Victorian woman who is *enceinte*. She received an immediate call to nonstop action. Her mothering began immediately. Wrote the French doctor André Théodore Brochard, "When a woman becomes pregnant she no longer belongs to herself. She belongs entirely to the being she carries within her, and whose existence has been trusted to her by God."

But fear not. The little tyrant who now owns your mind and body is a benign ruler. Though you will suffer much under his regime, your rewards will be manifold, especially if you handle this pregnancy as a Victorian woman would. There will be naps, oh so bounteous naps, no one snatching your brie, and of course you can still drink!

"HEY! I don't care how healthy it is or that the entire nation of Japan still eats it while pregnant, I OWN YOU and I said NO SUSHI!" —King Baby

Q: Stop. No. You most certainly cannot drink. That's injurious and foolish.

A: Absolutely. Allow me to legally state here that I do not encourage alcohol consumption while pregnant. To say otherwise would be just silly and a great big wide invitation for lawsuits.

But.

Waking up on the floor with no pants and a strange doll next to you: the tragic refrain of drunk babies.

You might be surprised to learn how recently drinking while pregnant became the grievous atrocity we now consider it. It was only toward the later end of the nineteenth century, during a health craze for abstention from all things stimulating, from pickles to porter, that drinking while pregnant became unpopular.

The editor of *American Motherhood* wrote in 1903 of the changing attitude toward drink: "The baby may sleep better because the mother drinks beer, but it is the semi-stupor of intoxication. In beer-drinking countries the physicians assert that among the women who are constant beer drinkers it is difficult to find a sober baby."

Even then the concern wasn't whether alcohol would impede a child's physical or mental development while in the womb or on the breast. The problem was you might breed a generation of dopey drunk little babies who would continue the habit into adulthood.

We know that constant consumption of alcohol is dangerous to both mother and baby. It's dangerous to anyone. But as for the threat of mild alcohol consumption causing birth defects, it may not be as high as you fear. A twenty-first-century study from the National Institute on Alcohol Abuse and Alcoholism estimated for every one thousand births in America, ten children will be born with alcohol-related birth defects. That is 1 percent, but it is a savage number no matter how small.

However, the NIAAA also studied risk factors for the mothers of these babies and found that most were already severely alcoholic before they were pregnant and carried their alcoholism into their pregnancy.

We're not talking about women who sip a glass of Pinot with a nice dinner late in their pregnancy, but people who are addicts and in severe distress. Westerners have never been good with moral gray areas, especially regarding babies. It's possible we abstain from occasional alcohol when pregnant today because we misunderstand the degree of danger it represents. Then again, we care so much for baby that we're willing to do, or not do, anything to give him even the smallest extra layer of protection.

Q: Didn't women of Victorian times feel the same way?

A: Well, yes, as much as they could. This is difficult to dwell on, so I'll try to be brief. Victorians, generally, tried not to grow as attached to their babies, born or unborn, as we do. No matter their rank or station, Victorians took it as a given that nearly everything in the world was lying in wait to snuff out the life of their baby, and that those evil forces would often succeed. It didn't mean those mothers loved any less, or cried any softer, or were any less broken when they miscarried from malnutrition and overwork, or lost a child to croup. It just means they weren't nearly as surprised.

There were so many threats to babies and pregnancies in the minds of the Victorian mother, from a rough carriage ride to being startled by an ugly nun. Wondering whether or not a drink of ale would hurt a fetus, well, that is a luxury people with plenty of clean water and reliable medical care get to suffer. Water, you must remember, was a crapshoot. Literally. Before the nineteenth century, drinking water very often shared underground tables with wastewater. The processes used to make alcohol killed much of the bacteria that caused cholera, dysentery, and countless other ills.

For most of Western history, pregnant women drank alcohol. Not to excess; a lady didn't want to appear a sloppy drunk. But beer, mead, ale, wine, and liqueurs were simply part of the human diet, as well as a much-relied-on medication.

Victorian women wanted to have safe pregnancies, same as us. It's just that back then...that probably included a goodly dose of malt liquor. In an 1858 edition of the medical journal *Transactions,* a Dr. D. L. M'Gugin wrote,

> *I have during the past year been highly gratified with the results of malt liquor, during pregnancy, as in lactation. Several patients who had been thin and emaciated, acquired not only strength and vigor, but were relieved of their sufferings. One lady who had lost three children during their infancy, and who was spare, thin, and pale, found herself pregnant for the fourth time. She became dejected...and was advised to use the malt beer, and in a short time found herself with more strength and health than ever before.*

Dr. M'Gugin explained that the patient put on weight, had a healthy birth, and was able to nurse her child for the first time, who in turn was growing strong.

The malt liquor the doctor recommended was of a "class of beer

"Golly, Sue, if your nerves are bad you should lay off the whiskey and smoke some nice soothing tobacco."

prepared from the hops, with a large amount of malt, and in an active state of effervescence. In this form we derive the benefits of the tonic properties of the hop, the nutrient principles of the malt, and the soothing qualities of the carbonic acid."

Q: So you recommend I take my prenatal vitamin with a forty of Schlitz?

A: I would like to remind you that sarcasm is the language of hate. Of course not. But I am telling you that for the entirety of history, all over the world, pregnant women have drunk alcohol in moderation and safely delivered children. I can understand if you don't feel comfortable joining their ranks. In fact, I should officially tell you not to. If for no other reason than you seem argumentative and litigious.

Besides, as we're about to learn, plain old alcohol was positively one of the most boring substances Victorians used to soothe the discomforts of pregnancy.

Q: What sort of discomforts? What did they use for medicine?

A: The list of minor complaints suffered by the expecting mother is near endless. Let me just focus on two of the more private concerns.

Constipation

We may not like to talk about it, but the inability to pass regular, comfortable poops can cause an already uncomfortable mother-to-be to feel like she literally has a stick up her posterior. Modern pregnant women are reluctant to take laxatives or stool softeners, lest the medication cause the baby to be born with runny poop (it will be) or a proclivity to play in toilet bowls (it's going to). There are many reasons a pregnant woman is subject to constipation. Less physical activity, increased progesterone slowing the movement of the digestive tract, and pressure of the womb on the lower intestine. Well, those are the current popular theories, anyway. Other causes have fallen to history, though they may be just as much to blame.

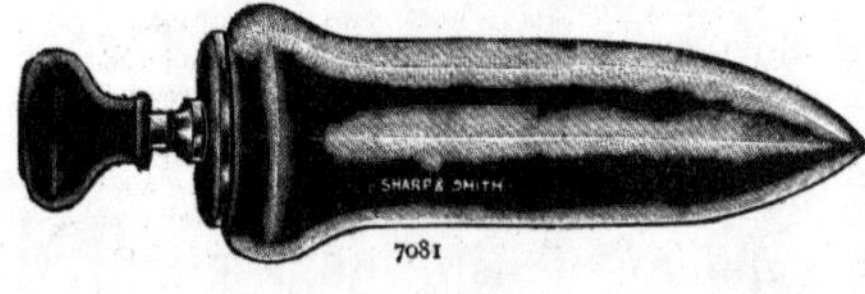

Dr. Pratt's Rectal Dilator for daily use to restore regularity, 1889.

The Water-Cure in Pregnancy and Childbirth, written by Joel Shew in 1849, blames this new "soft white flour" that's become all the rage. Which, unless you're a big hippie with a spelt fetish, is the basis of all the bread products you eat today. From Shew: "Superfine flour is, I hold, the greatest of all causes of constipation. No woman, if she can have brown bread, and occasionally an injection [enema], need ever suffer from constipation of the bowels."

John Epps, who wrote *Constipation: Its Theory and Cure* in 1854 (which he lovingly dedicated to his wife), doesn't think the problem is as simple as bread and biscuits. The reason pregnant women get constipated is because their uncontrolled sexual arousal is stealing the muscle power of the rectum.

> *The over-excitement of the genital organs by sexual or other excess, produces, by exhausting the nervous energy, a loss of expulsive power in the muscles of the rectum, thus causing the rectum not readily to respond to the stimulus of the fecal matter. Accumulations are thus caused in the rectum and constipation is manifested.*

And somewhere, Mrs. Epps sits with her face in her hands, caught between pride in her husband's publication and the shame of him subtly revealing to the world that she is horny and constipated.

As they are today, laxatives and purgatives were frowned upon during pregnancy. Doctors recommended "auxiliary" treatment. You're welcome to try enemas and rectal dilators, but the most common method of removing true fecal impaction is still the one used today. That is to say, a crooked finger. It's going to put up a fight, so be ready for that. It's like a coal deposit up there. And though we do not generally embrace modern methods on this journey to parenthood, you will find no judgment here if you choose to use the very modern invention of latex

"Auxiliary" treatment for severe constipation. You're probably going to want to roll up those sleeves.

gloves during the process. Or even those thick black rubber gloves that evil scientists wear in movies to handle plutonium.

Constipation is torment enough, but it is also one of the direct causes of our next affliction. Luckily, this one has a much less invasive treatment. Technically illegal, actually. But only by the laws of a meddlesome twenty-first-century government. Back in the day when people were trusted to care for themselves, a tetch of hemorrhoid heroin wasn't going to do anyone any harm.

Hemorrhoids

Don't strain so much—you're likely to pop a blood vessel! In your tushy. That's all hemorrhoids are, really: swollen and irritated blood vessels that poof up and protrude from the anus. The best Victorian cure comes from Mary Ries Melendy. Trust a lady doctor to prescribe treatments that don't fool around! She promises you'll find relief naturally, just by regularly "anointing" the afflicted area with a homemade tea made of chamomile and four poppy-heads.

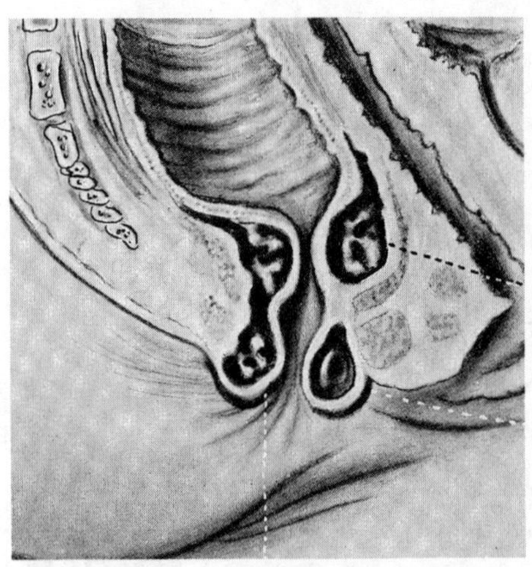

The most common varieties of hemorrhoids in pregnant women. Or, if you're squeamish, an aerial map of some islands in the South Pacific.

Q: That sounds pleasant enough. But I can't find "poppy-head tea" at the grocery store or pharmacy.

A: Oh, they're not usually stocked with the other teas. Pharmacies do have them, but they're in pill form now and they're called "opiates." Or have been given snazzy names like OxyContin, Percocet,

Demerol...even just plain old morphine! And—bonus—they are absorbed fantastically through rectal tissue! Even better than through oral ingestion, some modern studies say. And if your hemorrhoids are a real terror, there is a very powerful distillation of poppy-head extract that is called "heroin." It's extra refined so as to do its job extra well!

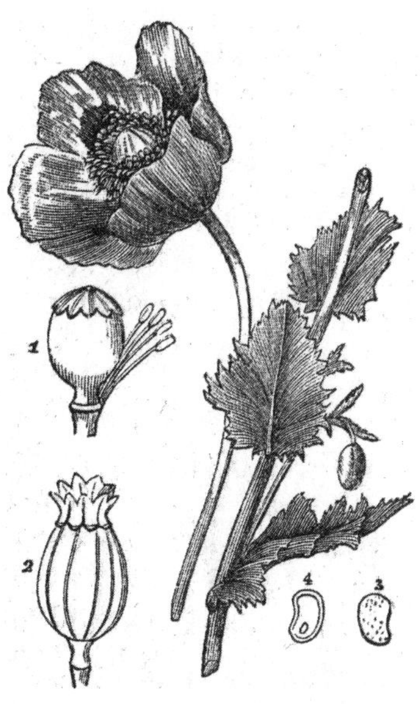

Poppy-heads, circa 1853.

Not many pharmacies carry that nowadays, though. You might need to go someplace else. I can't tell you exactly where, so it's a bit of a treasure hunt! Find the most decrepit part of any large city, and just wait around a bit after dark. You can ask passersby if they know where to buy some, but if you're lucky someone might walk right up and offer it to you! Bring cash. Modern heroin distributors are usually very firm on cash only.

Q: You want me to go to the city and ask around for heroin. I... I've been reading the back of the book and you're not remotely a doctor of any kind, are you?

Highly refined "black tar" poppy-heads as confiscated during a police raid, circa 2005.

A: Which is precisely why you need my unbiased perspective. Now, why would you balk at a small adventure like your search for uncut poppy dust? An expecting mother should be keeping her brain and body active!

Also, if police should approach you and ask your business, simply point to your belly and tell them you're pregnant and need heroin to rub on your swollen rectum.

Q: I'm sorry. I can't see that ending well. I'm going to use Preparation H.

A: You're just going to swagger into a drugstore and plop a tube of chemical anus cream on the counter for all to see, huh? I wouldn't imagine any self-respecting mother-to-be could be so brazen, but if you don't mind the stares, go right ahead. Just remember, your behavior is already imprinting on your baby, with potentially disastrous results.

Q: I mean, you have, like, no qualifications whatsoever that I can find...Back up. What do you mean, "imprinting with disastrous results"?

A: Your child, from the moment of conception, is exposed to every emotion, sound, sight, and thought you experience. And all of these things have an enormous impact on who they will become. Or as Melendy says: "That a mother may, during the period of gestation, exercise great influence, by her own mental and physical action, either unwittingly or purposely in such a way as to determine the traits and tendencies of her offspring, is now a common belief among all intelligent people."

You are capable of inflicting harm on your baby—worse harm than all the malt liquor and butt heroin in the world—just by going about your daily life. "There is no limit to the evil a mother may entail upon her unborn child; while on the other hand it is impossible to picture the happy results her efforts may accomplish."

This is what I meant when I said it is a mistake of the modern age to believe that your only task for the next nine months is balanced nutrition and learning to assemble an Ikea crib. Your perfect child (or degenerate monster) is forming from the power of your own mind from day one.

Q: That's really unsettling. How do I make my body a happy and nourishing place for my baby to grow?

A: First, surround yourself with beauty. The walls of your bedchamber should be filled with art that encourages noble contemplation. Pastoral scenes, nothing jarring. Try statuary. Send someone to that place that sells lawn statues and fill your room with pretty ladies pouring jars of water or babies peeing. Nothing distressing or ugly should cross your path. Under no circumstances should you expose yourself to dirty laundry piles or toilets that need cleaning.

You don't want to birth a child who relishes squalor, do you? This comes from Dr. John West, the author of *Maidenhood and Motherhood, or Ten Phases of a Woman's Life* in 1886:

> *[The pregnant woman's] chamber should have a southern exposure, if possible. This room should be kept free from all confusion of furniture, and, above all things, should have a cheerful look. If pictures and other ornamental works of art can be arranged about the walls, so much the better. Everything of a gloomy cast or suggestive of discomfort and disorder, should be carefully excluded. The mind of the wife will take on the impression of what the eyes reveal, and the state of the mind will be surely impressed upon the child's mind and disposition.*

Q: Think beautiful thoughts in a beautiful environment, birth beautiful baby. Got it.

A: You most certainly do not "got it" if you think it's that simple.

The "lying-in" room where Isaac Newton was born. Proving that to incubate a man of true distinction you may need to forgo the slavish luxury of a bed.

You only know of the things you must embrace, but the list of things you must avoid is ever so much more important. And longer! For instance, what do you think causes birthmarks, physical deformity, and children who grow up to be criminals?

Q: Various inherited and environmental factors, some of which are not yet completely understood?

A: No. Blame not God nor Nature for your own necromancy. They come from *your* body and *your* mind, Mother, specifically your lack of control over both.

A mother's emotions can be transmitted to the mind and body of the developing fetus. Listen to these examples of "Mother's Markings" or "Maternal Impressions," as reported by Thomas Shannon in 1904's *Nature's Secrets Revealed,* and by Edward Bliss Foote in 1889's *Plain Home Talk.*

And try not to be shocked by them; that will defeat the whole purpose.

- **Deformed Lip**—A pregnant woman fell into a violent passion; she bled at the nose, and wiping the blood from her lip, bore a child wanting a lip.
- **Form of Lizard on Breast**—A prospective mother became frightened at a lizard jumping into her bosom. She bore a child with an unnatural appendage exactly resembling a lizard, growing from its breast, adhering by the head and neck.
- **Fire Mark**—A woman, absent from home, became alarmed by seeing a large fire in the direction of her own house, and bore a child with a distinct mark of a flame upon its forehead.
- **Bear Baby**—A woman gave birth to a child covered with hair, and having the claws of a bear. This was attributed to her beholding the images and pictures of bears hung up in the palace of the Ursini family, to which she belonged.
- **Lobster Craving**—A woman who had longed for a lobster, brought forth a child resembling one of those animals.

Q: C'mon. Most newborns look a little like lobsters. Squashed lobsters.

A: Shhh! Can you continue your flippancy in the face of this tragic tale told by Dr. West? He tells us of a pregnant woman who was

> *compelled to pass a grog-shop, and as she came to it she heard a voice that was strangely like her husband's, singing a ribald song. She was so struck with astonishment*

> *that she involuntarily looked in at the door. She beheld her husband in a state of hilarious intoxication. This was but a few weeks before the birth of her child.*

Lo and behold, the baby grew into a toddler with all the characteristics of a drunkard. The child, he tells us, had no coordination in the movements of the lower limbs. "The child's gait was heavy and insecure—a regular drunken reel or stagger. The speech was not only thick, incoherent, and rambling, but had all the phenomena of exhilaration and excitement characteristic of the earlier stages of intoxication."

Q: There seem to be a lot of drunk babies in this book.

A: And we're only in Chapter 2, my friend.

Q: Aren't babbling and stumbling fairly standard behavior for toddlers?

A: This wasn't the normal babbling incoherent clumsiness of a two-year-old. This was the babbling incoherent clumsiness of a two-year-old bearing a mother's mark and a father's shame. For you see: "It is one of the most singular cases on record, and can be accounted for on no other hypothesis than that the impression of horror made on the mother's mind [by the soused husband] was conveyed to the fetus within her womb."

Q: See, I don't think he quite gets what "hypothesis" means. Does he explain how this transference of drunkenness occurred?

A: Of course. It happened through the little-understood witchery of electricity. And daguerreotypes. That, my friend, is an old-fashioned term for "photography."

Foote explains:

> *The fright, annoyance, or whatever it may be, produces a sudden accumulation in the brain of the*

*"*Hic*...this is the gal. I love this gal.
C'mere, ya *hic* big silly."*

> *electrical forces of the nervous system, and a sudden propulsion of them to all parts of the system, including the uterus, where the local currents are interfered with by the intrusion of the more powerful and instantaneous currents from the brain, bearing a daguerreotype of the object or subject which causes the fright or annoyance.*

Now couple this with the mysterious properties of blood. Dr. Shannon explains,

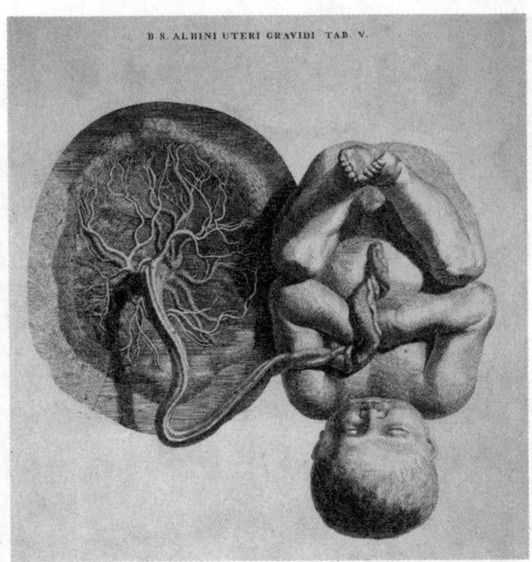

Baby and placenta, which is apparently mostly ornamental.

> *Only a very delicate membrane separates the vital fluid of the mother from that of the infant in her womb. There is a constant interchange of the blood in its body with that in hers through this exceedingly thin membrane, and thus all nervous impressions which have produced an alteration of either a temporary or permanent character in the circulating fluid of the mother are communicated to the child.*

Q: I thought the placenta kept the blood of the mother and the baby separate?

A: If that were so then the above wouldn't make much sense, would it? Plus, it would put holes in our theory as to why honorable women will sometimes have children that bear no resemblance to their husbands.

Dr. Foote reports more about the strange miracle of Maternal Impression.

> *Prof. Britton tells us of a lady who lived in Fairfield County, Conn., and in universal esteem for her exemplary life and unblemished character but who gave birth to a child who seemed to almost perfectly resemble the minister presiding over the church of which she was a member. The child has become a tall and graceful youth, and yet resembles the parson.*
>
> *Professor Simpson, of Edinburgh, gives an instance of a young woman of that city, born of white parents, whose mother, some time previous to her marriage, had a child by a mulatto man-servant, and this young lady exhibits distinct traces of the negro. Her hair, particularly, resembles that of the African.*

Q: Ha...ha...how does science explain these children who strongly resemble men not their mother's legal husband? Because I've got a guess.

A: Magnets.

Q: Totally.

A: You're curious, of course, how that is possible.

Q: Oh, yeah. Bring it.

A: Well, in the case of the child looking like his mother's handsome pastor, that's another case of imprinting. The pastor, like a sculpture or painting, was a thing of beauty that greatly stirred the passions of the mother.

Q: Heh...I bet he did.

A: *But*...(if I may continue) in the case of the child bearing a resemblance to a previous lover, Dr. Foote explains the culprit is magnetism: "The womb becomes magnetized and, in many cases, permanently, by the male in copulation, and the individual magnetism so imparted to the womb, causes the organ to exercise an important influence upon the mental and physical character of the growing embryo which it contains."

Friction, you see, creates magnetism. Like when you rub a balloon on your hair, or a penis in your vagina. Foote explains that the womb is then struck with the magnetism of the male, and if he is a very magnetic man, his presence will imprint on the babies of other men growing in the womb.

And if logic alone cannot convince you, behold this thrilling tale related by one Dr. Davis:

> *A woman of considerable physical courage, mounted a horse, rode side by side with her soldier-husband, and witnessed the drilling of the troops for battle. The exciting music and scene together inspired her with a deep thirst to behold a war and a conquest. This event transpired a few months before the birth of her child, whose* name was—Napoleon.

Oh, yes. *That* Napoleon. Mrs. Bonaparte took a keen interest in battle and gave the world one of the fiercest military strategists in history.

Q: Didn't Napoleon end up losing big, though? He died alone, banished, in exile?

A: That's not the poi— Oh, I'm sorry. Here, let's take a moment and you can tell me *your* battle plan for defeating the British and Prussians at Waterloo. I'm sure it will far surpass Emperor Bonaparte's. The point is he was a military genius. And you're not. So hush.

"And I woulda gotten away with it, too, if it weren't for those meddling Brits."

Q: So. This magnetized brain-blood that…photobombs your baby with "Maternal Impressions" business seems quite dire. Are there other dangers that might imprint on my child?

A: Take care to avoid unpleasant people. Nor can you yourself ever be unpleasant.

Or as Melendy puts it,

> *It hardly seems necessary in this connection to advert to the importance of avoiding all exercise of malevolent feelings, such as anger, envy, jealousy, hatred, revenge, covetousness, or wrong desire of any nature, which, if indulged, may implant in the embryo the subtle germs, from which will grow in after years the bitterest fruits.*

"You know your wretched attitude toward life is the reason I'm short, don't you, Mother?"

The experts agree you should avoid socializing with twits and grouchy crosspatches for the sake of your babe. Also people with unsightly moles. Stubby fingers. Hay fever so that they're constantly sniffing in the most grating manner. Secretly we have all suspected God doesn't curse people with dry skin or tuberculosis unless there is a deep vein of sin running through their hearts. And this very-nearly-science proves such depravity can be imparted unto your unborn child through association.

Says Dr. Foote, "Association with deformed people, or those having birth-marks, or diseases which cause unnatural manifestations and expressions, should be avoided so far as practicable, to avert the danger of marking the unborn child with any of these peculiarities."

In fact, continues Foote, it's a crying shame that those...*sorts*... are allowed in public at all.

Accidents will occasionally happen to shock the nerves of pregnant women, but deformed people should be kept out of public thoroughfares: "[The pregnant woman] ought especially to turn away her eyes from those hideous deformities which are met with often in the streets of our great cities, where they should not be allowed to display themselves."

Q: All right, this is not just crazy but it's also mean, and my resulting irritation is going to imprint on my fetus. Can we talk about something more prosaic? Like, what were the maternity clothing options in Victorian times?

A: It's a funny thing. Victorian society is thrilled you're pregnant, truly. But they don't want to have to *look* at it. If women were able, they often went into "confinement" toward the end of their terms, not just for health reasons, but for the sake of appearance. Yes, you're glowing and all that but you're also a grotesquely swollen reminder of the animalistic rutting nature that humans just can't seem to get away from. Look at you, waddling down the street, a veritable billboard for sexual incontinence. Just, ew. No. Go home.

Note the slight lift of the hem in the front of the gown, a small sure sign of pregnancy. Note getting photographed while pregnant, a sure sign of being shameless.

For most women of the era, maternity clothes were called "clothes." Many women stitched in "pregnancy panels" to give their dresses and skirts more girth, or, if a woman expected her pregnancies to come with regularity, simply sewed her clothes with many extra inches of seam allowance that she could "let out" as she grew. Under special circumstances a woman of means who for whatever reason could not stay in confinement might commission fancy maternity wear that strove to hide the embarrassing details of her pregnant shape through extensive draping, turning her into a silky, waddling land barge.

It wouldn't be until the early twentieth century, when a Lithuanian immigrant in dire need of cash discovered an untapped market, that the first official "maternity dress" would be designed and sold. Lena Bryant, a widow supporting herself and her young son as a seamstress, was approached by clients who needed clothes that allowed them to be both pregnant and outside of the house.

The middle class born of the industrial age had created thousands of women who needed to do their own shopping, errands,

Lena (Lane) Bryant.

and even work outside the home while pregnant. Lena designed a dress with an elasticized waistband and an accordion-pleated skirt, which was technically the first-ever mass-produced maternity dress. In 1904 she took out a bank loan and opened a shop on Fifth Avenue. The bank employee misspelled her name on the loan application, and the error stuck.

At first Lane Bryant wasn't allowed to advertise its special design, since reference to pregnancy in print was indecent. Her first advertisement didn't run until 1911. Her stock sold out the next day. It was some years later that Lena, after measuring the body dimensions of her customer base, addressed another underserved segment of the population, "the Stout." She sold her clothes for larger ladies from a mail-order catalog for decades. Eventually Lane Bryant dropped maternity wear from its repertoire, instead focusing on becoming what is today the nation's number one plus-size fashion chain, with 775 storefronts, 10,000 employees, and quarterly revenues in the $200 millions. It seems "fitting" that the woman who was among the first to recognize pregnant women as actual people would lead the charge in affording "stout" women the same courtesy.

Q: What about underwear? The Victorians were quite finicky about proper undergarments, weren't they?

A: The only really tricky thing about underclothing, remembering that the Victorians favored loose chemises and drawstring drawers, were corsets. It's important to remember that corsets weren't used for vanity alone in centuries past. They were support garments, used to

Lane Bryant made clothes both for the mother-to-be and the figure-that-results.

keep the many parts of the adult female torso that tend to flap and slap secured in place. But how to continue to do so while not squishing your tiny tummy tag-along?

André Brochard outlined how important it was for the expectant mother to forgo modesty, at least regarding the baby bump: "Clothes of a pregnant woman ought to be ample, not tight, and they should in no way prevent the development of the abdomen, or that of the child. The stays [corset] should be loosely laced, and composed of simple elastic materials, with only one purpose, and that is, to sustain the breasts."

One of the ways to counteract the offensive imagery of pregnancy was to display maternity corsets on models so slim they couldn't have birthed gerbils.

But, Brochard cautioned, be careful with the breasts, too. You don't want to push your nipples inside out. You're going to need those. "Attention is to be paid lest the nipples be compressed by the stays. The depression of the nipples, which sometimes makes suckling so painful for both mother and child, is often solely due to this cause."

Melendy suggested you do more than protect those little suckers...use this time to prepare your milk muskets for battle!

> *To Harden the Nipples—A mother sometimes suffers severely from sore nipples. Such suffering may frequently be prevented, if for six weeks or two months before confinement, the nipples are bathed for five minutes every night and morning, either with merigold ointment or with equal parts of brandy and water.*

For most of the 1800s a woman was able to buy a "maternity" or "hygienic" corset for her pregnancy. This usually consisted of a corset with extra lacing above the hips, to allow growth, as well as breast cups that could by flipped down for nursing.

Q: What did Victorians expect a husband to do to help his wife's pregnancy along?

A: He's already done it! Filled your indolent womb with the serum of life! What more do you want of the poor man? It is true that the particularly indulgent husband can be a great help during a pregnancy. Melendy urges men to "smooth her rugged path, shade her from the burning flame of mental agitation, encourage her, and when the time comes that she lies prostrated, her face beaming with happiness at the sound of her first-born, thank God that you have been kind to her." It might be wise for the husband to put extra emphasis on the "shade her from the burning flame of mental agitation" part. A pregnant woman's brain is just a sloshing swamp of hormones and emotions and temporary insanity. But a loving husband will tolerate it. Dr. West reminds husbands:

Indulging the pregnant wife. Like a hat's gonna make that gut look any smaller, but don't tell her that.

> *It is always desirable to gratify the woman. These are but whims, of course, but where their gratification does no harm, it is best to humor them. It tranquilizes the mind. The whole aim should be to prevent the wife brooding over any matter, however trivial or foolish it may seem to the husband. He must remember that she is not herself, and must be as patient and forebearing with her as with a feeble child.*

Q: Treat your wife like a feeble child. Huh. That is the *literal* definition of being "patronizing." I guess if you're going to treat your wife like a feeble child, no more sex, then, huh?

A: Don't be so petty and indignant—that's precisely how a feeble child would react. As for marital relations, thinking is divided on this. Everyone agrees restraint should be exercised, but completely denying either partner sexual intercourse could have repercussions.

Dr. Brochard, who, I might remind you again, is a Frenchman, flat out says sex should continue during pregnancy: "The rights of the husband ought not to be suspended during the pregnancy of the wife, but moderation in these is necessary."

Dr. Foote, however, worries that sexual excess, or even a persistent sexual desire on the part of the mother, will cause you to birth a little Frenchm—ah...pervert: "During the period of pregnancy, excessive sexual indulgence unduly develops, in the unborn child, the passion which leads so many young people to a destructive vice. Even amative excitement, on the part of the mother, without indulgence, has a tendency to do this."

He recommends she avoid spicy food and other sexual triggers, as well as sleeping in a separate bed from her husband. However, if there's just no putting her off, "when the impulse becomes strong—when the desire is so great as to take possession of the mind, it is then better that it should be gratified, lest the foetus be marked by this unsatisfied appetite, thereby producing the very evil sought to be avoided."

If she's got to have it, no matter how bloated and whiny she is, it's your duty as a man of honor and as a future father to give it up. You're having sex for two now. Three, even, if you include your wife as a person.

How fast these nine months fly with so much to concentrate on. The hour of birth approaches...well...many, many hours, probably. Grab your midwife, chloroform, and rubber sheets. Here comes the Little Stranger.

3

If Suffering in Birth Is Ordained by God, May I Bite a Towel During Delivery Without Offending Him?

On the Occasionally Fatal Privilege of Childbirth

How to position a "very fat" woman for birth.
Hopefully she is also a yoga master.

Now it is time to talk about your "birth plan." Where you attempt to arrange and micromanage one of the most chaotic events of your life into something akin to a structured Napa Valley wine tour. You may choose the place you wish to give birth, who shall be your attendant, what pain control methods you'll use, and who you want in the room during the event.

Perhaps your unique plan details that your home birth will take place in a converted antique horse trough placed in your front yard, where the air is redolent with your posies and spice garden. And if the Hendricksons next door don't like it they can close their dang curtains. The trough will be filled with a combination of fresh spring water and ashwagandha herbs imported from Sri Lanka. Don't let anyone try to argue you out of it: this is all about you.

It is perfectly reasonable to require that your partner join you in stripping naked, and it will also be his/her responsibility to wave the purifying burning sage around your belly and delicately swab your damp brow with natural sponge from the Mediterranean Sea. You've heard that orgasms are one of the most powerful natural painkillers, and your partner is game to try. His parents should be honored to be there, and it's certainly not your problem if they aren't prepared to watch his attempts to comfort you. There is no place for shame in your birth plan!

You have scheduled three to five hours for labor, to be broken up with a light catered brunch. Once the child is born she shall be received and blessed by your college roommate Lisa, who is now a Wic-

Some birth plans demand more tree bark and whimsy than others.

can priestess, then swaddled in the manner traditional to Tibetan newborns. Remember to butter his head for luck.

And that is precisely how it's going to happen. Who dares defy you and your meticulous preordination? Not me, certainly. But of course God, Nature, your own forthcoming child…I can't speak for them.

They all have a long history of disrespecting the most carefully laid plans.

Q: Stop making fun of that stuff. A woman *does* have freedom—it's her body and her birth experience. And I think replicating a cozy Victorian home birth would be wholesome and soothing. No cold, antiseptic hospital. No being pumped full of dangerous drugs. Childbirth is not an illness.

A: Yeah. You *say* that…

Puerperal pyrexia, placental abruption, placenta previa, general uterine hemorrhaging, eclampsia.

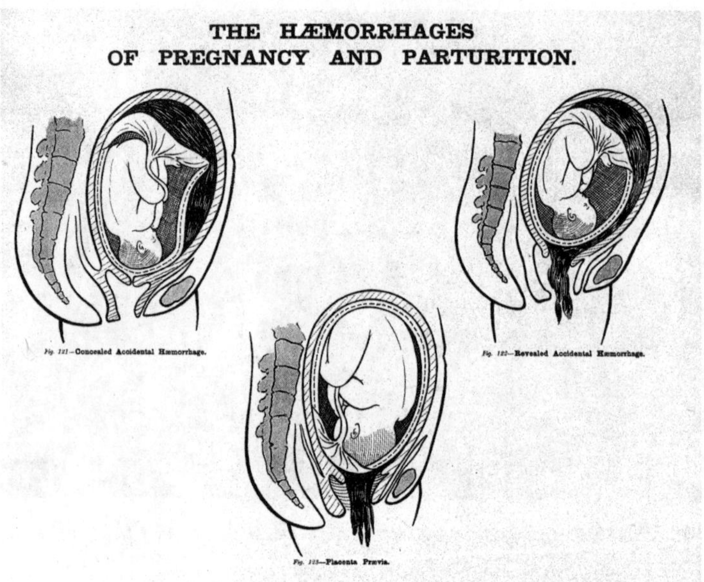

The black stuff...that's your blood. It's not in the right place and it's not going to stop.

Q: What are those?

A: Childbirth illnesses. No...that's the wrong word. More "agonizing complications of childbirth that end in boiled fever brain and/or blood-soaked death." And that's just what a Victorian version of *you* would risk during birth. I won't tell you the things that could happen to your baby. Just two words. *More,* and *worse.*

Let me say this before we proceed. Have your baby at home, if you wish. Or in one of those Bed & Breakfast & Babies birthing centers. Have the child in a natural mineral warm spring at a posh ski resort! The ski resort might not like it but let's see them try to move you once you've started. For pain control, use only breathing techniques, or suck on ice chips imported from an Alaskan glacier blessed by an Inuit shaman. Be attended by an unlicensed midwife, doula, or your gay best friend from high school who is sick of his dental practice and is thinking of branching out. He makes everything feel like a party!

But listen to me, please. Whatever you do, have that child within a ten-minute ambulance ride of the biggest, most frigidly modern and antiseptic hospital you can find. One filled with terrifying operating rooms, impersonal but spot-on professional medical teams, and every knock-out, hemorrhage-staunching, flesh-repairing, life-giving drug and tool of the modern age.

Because you're right, childbirth isn't an illness. But it can turn into an irreversible tragedy within seconds. Victorian women knew that better than anyone. Take every precaution so that you never need know the terror and grief they knew.

Q: Yeah, well...okay. I was planning that anyway. A contingency plan is just common sense. Come to think about it, women do die a lot in childbirth in Victorian stories.

A: They probably didn't die as much as fiction would have us believe. Removing a mother from a narrative immediately frees up a romantic male lead or gives the young heroine access to freedoms and dangers she wouldn't face under a mother's protection. If literature retained its mothers, there would be no adventures for Tom and Huck, Catherine wouldn't have run wild with Heathcliff on the moors, Sarah Crewe would never have been shut up in the attic by Miss Minchin, there'd be no need for a Secret Garden, and even Quasimodo would have lived his life in some faraway hut in the woods instead of consorting with gypsies and jumping lithely through the architecture of Notre-Dame. In reality, it's hard to compile records for deaths in childbirth from the nineteenth century, but what data there is suggests there were, at any given point, between forty and seventy maternal deaths per one thousand

The unprofessional and unpleasant midwife grumbles toward her work.

births. *Maternal* deaths, not infant deaths. Those were excruciatingly higher.

Q: I feel comfortable wanting a midwife instead of a doctor. They're licensed today, well trained, and are more intimate with their client. I want a lady one, in fact.

A: Well, then your timing is remarkably off! Anytime before this era there would be no *question* that you would be attended by a well-reputed female midwife. With few exceptions, men of all cultures avoided participation in childbirth throughout history. In fact, even today obstetricians and midwives are overwhelmingly female. But in the Victorian era, men slowly took over childbirth, and owned it for the next century and a half.

Q: Oh, that is so typical. How'd the Penisocracy manage to hijack the most sacred tradition of womanhood?

A: I think you made that word up, and I like it, though it's rather harsh. A lot of things contributed to the temporary death of the female midwife. But like so many things in the nineteenth century, it can be partly traced back to machines.

Machines were labor-saving devices, creating leisure time for those who could afford it. Leisure created curiosity, which led to study, building new machines, performing experiments, and sharing information through publications. Men looked around and found that due to the heretofore absence of the learned male mind, the study of female physiology was sorely lacking.

Male doctors began to usurp midwives by presenting themselves as more educated and sanitary than their female counterparts. Men went to college and published scholarly articles in medical journals. Midwives did not. Wealthy and important men read these journals and secured their writers to care for their wives. What wealthy folks do, middle-class folks want to do. And since doctors were popping up everywhere all of a sudden, it wasn't hard to procure one. Midwives couldn't compete, and doctors helped edge them out with publications decrying the filthy, ignorant state of the midwife.

In an 1890 editorial to the *North American Practitioner* periodical, a doctor argued the necessity of making obstetric care more available to the impoverished, in hope of doing away with midwifery:

> *Many of these midwives dabble in gynecology as well: they fit supporters, replace "turned wombs," etc., and not a few do a flourishing abortion business. Physicians unanimously declare their obstetrical work as a whole to be careless, and that their mortality from septic puerperal diseases is higher than it ought to be.*

In 1894, in the *New York Journal of Gynecology and Obstetrics,* Dr. William Pryor wrote that the proper training and registration of midwives had met with resistance in America and England because "it will be conceded that a supply of trained midwives will cut into the practice of a certain class of physicians very seriously."

But, he says, to let midwives run free as they are is tantamount to mass murder.

> *That many women are ruined by sepsis and other faults of midwives, that many die, that many children are still-born owing to imperfect methods of delivery are facts well known by every physician of experience in New York.... the midwife [is an] unclean, untrained old woman who seeks this way to make a living merely because she can not gain one in any other channel. The deathrate in New York is higher than it should be because of the ministrations of these ignorant creatures.*
>
> *If the mortality among women confined by midwives be too high, who may count those who have survived and remain chronic invalids as the result of infection directly due to the filthy methods of midwives!*

Doctors didn't want midwives trained and licensed because that would cut into their business. Not that it mattered much anyway; women who had to work outside the home for a living at that time were largely illiterate and would have had no time or support to receive formal education and licensing. So it was easy to paint the unlicensed midwifes as dirty, careless hags.

So, slowly, the penis-wielders won the day.

Of course, not everyone thought this was a good thing. In the earlier part of the century, before anyone, doctor or midwife, needed licensing, many people thought the entry of men into obstetrics was a travesty of indecency.

Q: Because a man couldn't be trusted to attend a woman's privates without being sexually stimulated? By a big mucus-plugged cervix?

A: What happened to the righteous indignation toward the Penisocracy? Now you *want* a male doctor?

Q: I just want options. It bugs me that people made such sweeping generalizations on who was a good attendant based on gender.

A: They didn't just base it on *gender*. They also considered what race you were, where your parents came from, how nice your house was, how often you were seen at church, and how far your family pew was toward the front *in* that church.

The Man-Midwife, *by Samuel Fores.*

What we call bigotry today was called Tuesday back then.

And, yes, it was feared that men were too lascivious to explore a pregnant woman's body. The movement toward male midwives, or *accoucheurs* (French for "an aide in childbirth" with a masculine suffix), was not a popular one in its early days. In fact, many found the idea quite obscene.

There's a certain logic to it. I mean, if nothing else, the fact that a woman is pregnant is proof that she puts out, amirite?

Q: Oooh. I am giving you such a scowl.

A: Seriously, it was a tradition started by a French whore, at least according to people who hated male midwives. A really famous *king's* whore, but still, a woman who had little regard for modesty. One Dr. Davis of London was quoted in John Stevens's 1849 work *Man-Midwifery Exposed, or The Danger and Immorality of Employing Men in Midwifery Proved; and the Remedy for the*

Evil Found, detailing how this strumpet laid the seeds for a wicked new trend in obstetrics.

Louise de La Vallière, the rumored Mother of Man-Midwifery and also a couple of royal French bastards.

> *It is pretty generally known that the Duchess of Villiers, a favourite mistress of Louis XIV, of France, was the first female who was induced to place herself under the exclusive obstetric care of a professor of surgery, independent of any anticipated necessity for a surgical operation. That event took place in December, 1665; and Julien Clement, the fortunate attendant upon the case, was soon after appointed to the most lucrative office of Midwifer to the Princess of France.*

Stevens clarifies why this signifies the end of all that is good and pure in childbirth: "How very few ladies, for a moment, suspect that, when their pride admits the favourite M.D. from his carriage to their closet, they are following the blighting treason first committed against that sacred, that universal modesty God gave to all creatures, by a Court prostitute of Paris!"

Think about it: If you invite a man not your husband into your bedroom and allow him to insert parts of his body into your most private areas, well, you're describing prostitution. Especially when you add how you'll be all sweaty and moaning and writhing, soaking the sheets with sexy amniotic fluid and trying to not defecate.

Actually Stevens, quoting a man known only as "a modern doctor," can describe the scene better than I.

> *His looking sedate or even demure [cannot] alter his natural impulses.... If he be in health and vigour of constitution, can he enter a chamber, and there find a pretty young woman waiting his arrival, and proceed, in privilege of custom, with bated breath, and insinuating manner, to ask questions relating to her interesting condition; proceed next to take what freedom with her naked person he pleases to think necessary, to find out if she is six weeks or three months gone, and to know if with child or not.*

Yeah. That's hot.

Q: Oh, gag me with a speculum.

A: Gross. Doctors were of course quick to defend themselves and utilize approaches that would provide the least amount of awkwardness. Dr. Karl Schroeder, in his 1873 *A Manual of Midwifery*, says the best way to break the ice with a lady whose vagina you're about to put your finger in is to just get to business.

> *Before examining internally no long discourse is necessary in order to prove to the woman the necessity of such an examination; let him show that it is necessary to do it by simply asking for some oil or cold cream, some water and a towel. If he examines her without many preliminaries he will not meet with any resistance or refusal on her part, since a woman who sends for the accoucheur must be prepared to be examined. He must,*

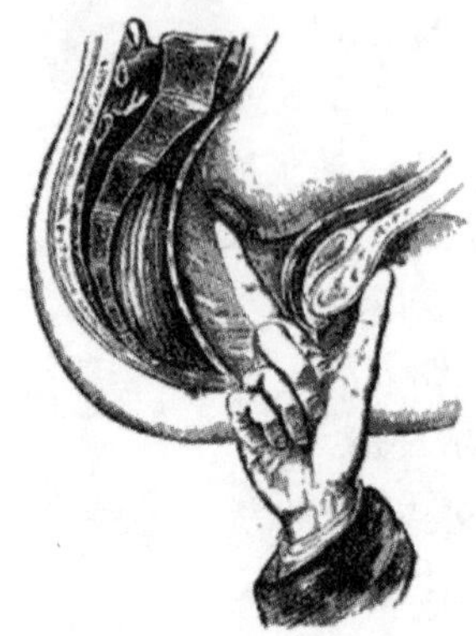

Galabin calls this method "The Shocker"! BOOP!

of course, proceed with all possible decency, but on no account whatever must he omit any method of examination if he considers it necessary.

Here Schroeder is setting a businesslike tone for the examination, giving the woman the benefit of the doubt that she is not a blushing child but a mother-to-be fully capable of distinguishing medical care from molestation.

Alfred Lewis Galabin, who wrote his own 1896 edition of *A Manual of Midwifery,* had another way of avoiding awkwardness during exams. The trick is to give the old girl a quick finger-jab right in the middle of her contraction: "It is usual and preferable to commence the examination during a pain, and hence arises the common phrase of 'taking a pain.' Her attention being distracted by the pain, the patient does not notice so much the inconvenience of the introduction of the examining finger."

Boom. Womb inspected, over and done, before the lady has time to process if she just got internally goosed.

Q: Okay, I have my midwife. How would the actual at-home birth take place?

A: Preparation first.

- **The Air**—Start a fire, as sweating helps birth. I imagine it just puts you in a frame of mind where you're happy to excrete things out of even the tiniest of openings. If you live in a home new enough to have an attached water closet, make sure to use a towel to stop up the gap under the door. The miracle of the U-bend had perhaps not quite been perfected, and it was of utmost importance that gases seeping up from sewers and septic tanks didn't enter the birth chamber, especially since a lot of attendants wouldn't let you open the windows for the next two weeks.

- **The Bed**—Lay something waterproof between your sheet and mattress. "Oil-cloth" (cloth boiled in linseed oil) was a favorite of the era, though if that could not be had, a nice thick layer of newspapers pinned to the mattress would do in a pinch, as would a rubber sheet, folded blanket, or "Turkish towels" (a large cloth made from the particularly absorbent weave of cotton or linen popular in Turkish baths, the precursor to bath towels).
- **The People**—Kick out everyone who isn't necessary. Your friends and your family and *especially* Auntie Gert, who

"Quick, lasses! Bridget is aboyt ter 'av a sprog an' needs our 'elp!"

last birthed a baby during the reign of Catherine the Great but still thinks she knows everything about the process and keeps trying to bleed off your sanguine humors with a fish-scaling knife...gone. No crowding. We're looking at you, Irishwomen. (Per Galabin: "With the poorer classes the attendant should insist that no more persons than necessary are in the room, since, especially among the Irish, the neighbours are fond of gathering in the lying-in room.") You can have a friend, but they must be the right sort, obnoxiously cheerful and not squeamish.

- **Your Personal Hygiene**—It is about to be grossly neglected, so the Connecticut Training School for Nurses 1878 edition of *A Hand-Book of Nursing for Family and General Use* advises its students to try to tend to as much as possible before labor begins in earnest.

> *[The nurse] should assist her in undressing, brush her hair,—for this cannot be done again for several days,—bandage the limbs if varicose veins be troublesome, and allow her to eat and drink freely of easily-digested food and unstimulating fluids. The best food is soup and beef-tea, and farinaceous dishes; the best drink simply cold water.*

Q: I'm grateful they're willing to let me eat and drink...modern maternity nurses are real jerks about that. But why can't I brush my hair after giving birth?

A: Phhffff. Pick a reason. Womb wobble? Milk bewitchment? Vanity-based sin scarring? Because nineteenth century, that's why.

Continuing with your preparations. As for what you should wear, the sports bra and long socks option popular today was not available. Alfred Lewis Galabin asked women to not act as the lower classes do, wearing a full dress and corset throughout the labor, as this would "often prove inconvenient." His suggested birth couture was as such:

> *It is preferable for the patient to be in her night-dress, over which she may wear a dressing-gown in the earlier stages of labour. It is a good plan for her also to wear underneath the night-dress a special petticoat, fastened loosely round the waist. The night-dress can then be tucked up and kept clean during delivery, and, when the labour is over, the soiled petticoat can be easily slipped off, and the necessity for changing the night-dress avoided.*

Other writers remind the woman to wear (thigh-high) stockings, and a few see no reason for her to remove her (open-crotched) drawers, especially if the weather is brisk. They aren't too specific about accessorizing, but it seems only good manners to make an effort to match your hat and gloves and handbag to the curtains.

Your Mother-Bits—Even if they don't believe in that bizarre new "germ theory" circulating through the medical community, your birth attendants are going to make an effort at cleanliness. For instance, they know you're going to want to poop, and they are determined that you shan't. The Connecticut Training School for Nurses is quite firm about pooping.

> *Above all, the midwife must remember that the patient's desire to defecate is due to the pressure of the foetal head upon the rectum, and under no circumstance may she be allowed to sit upon the night-chair*

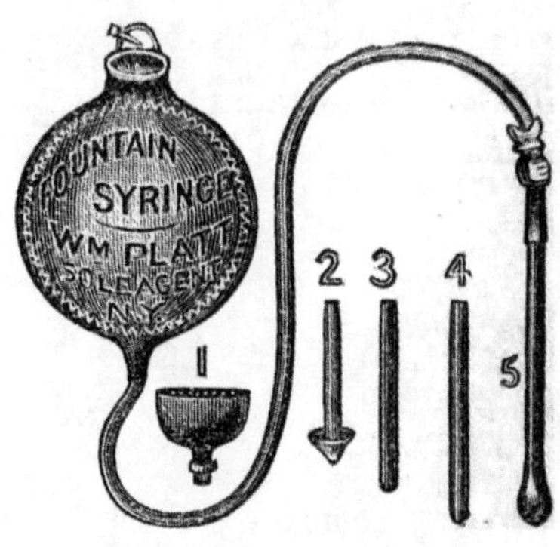

Fountain syringe with multiple attachments for both enemas and vaginal douching.

[chamber pot], since there is danger that the foetus also may be expelled, and injury to the mother and child follow.

Q: They worried…I'd…poop out the baby?

A: I know, if only it were that easy, right? But then again, some of these women were on their ninth or sixteenth delivery…for them it probably was best to pace themselves. Anyway, to prevent this, a non-negotiable part of childbirth was the enema and strenuous vaginal cleansing. The enemas usually contained fairly innocuous mixtures. Warm soapy water, emulsion of "slippery elm," "chamomile-tea," or "warm water with two teaspoonfuls of oil, and a teaspoonful of salt." Repeat as necessary. Your birth canal, however—that needed to be more than clean, especially as the later part of the century brought out the OCD in the entire Western world. You needed a pelvic floor you could eat off of.

And sometimes you'd need special tools for the occasion, as advised by *The Surgical Assistant* by Walter Brickner in 1905:

> *The assistant scrubs the [vaginal] canal with soap and water. For this purpose he may use a jeweler's brush. This has no bristles at the tip, and therefore hardly cleanses the presenting surface of the cervix; moreover, the bristles may lacerate the vaginal mucosa. It is better therefore, in most cases, to use a sea-sponge or gauze mop mounted in the tip of a clamp or pair of dressing forceps.*

Look at that! I guess your Victorian birth plan *can* include all-natural sea sponge!

Many doctors did not think soap and water were antiseptic enough to purify the birth canal. For brand names, Listerine was a reliable douche, or, as instructed by the Connecticut Training School for Nurses, "Many patients require to have the vulva washed in a weak solution of the carbolic acid and glycerine,—a tablespoonful to a quart of water, to prevent the action of decomposed discharges so common at this time."

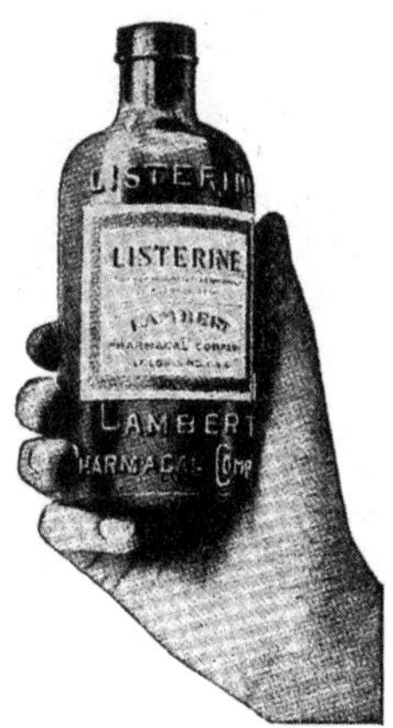

Listerine is way more versatile than we give it credit for. It can freshen lots more than just your mouth.

Q: So to keep me from accidentally *pushing* the baby out too fast, they intend to *blast* it out?

A: That's *nitro*glycerine. And carbolic acid isn't explosive. Well, it is, of course, but the circumstances have to be just right, so, hey, don't worry about it. It's not a pleasant concoction, but it will end with you having the tidiest undercarriage in town! For a few minutes, anyway…cuz a bunch of your insides and a baby are coming through.

Q: You're such a comfort. Not that I intend to use them, but what sort of medications were used to ease delivery in the Victorian era?

A: I will answer this, but I'll need to be dealing with an open mind. If you go all "I'm not getting chloroformed or dropping acid while pregnant," then we can't really have a fruitful discussion abo—

Q: I am NOT getting chloroformed or…Did you say *dropping acid?* Are you serious?

A: It wasn't dropping acid per se…it's ingesting the rotten rye grains, contaminated with the bacteria ergot, which is the natural

Rye grain with ergot (dark thorny growths) protruding.

source of the drug LSD. It was super hard to portion out right—you couldn't tell just how much the grain was infected. Too much and you experienced mania, psychosis, and hallucinations, and often died in a brutal seizure. Full disclosure, that *did* happen a few times in history, on a plague level, killing thousands when a community's crops got contaminated. They called the mysterious disease St. Anthony's Fire, but they didn't figure out what caused it until the mid-1800s. But, in the *right amounts,* this early ancestor of LSD caused a constriction of blood vessels and muscles that could both hasten labor and help slow postpartum bleeding.

The chloroform...yeah...just what you're thinking. "Stuff you in the trunk of a battered 1978 Lincoln Continental in the Mojave Desert and speed toward the border" sort of chloroform.

Q: I'm still stuck on the LSD. They fed the mothers...LSD.

A: Not really. It wasn't refined synthetic LSD like we have today. Actually, since it was only the crushed-up poisoned rye, it was just "LS," lysergic acid. The "D" didn't show up until 1938 when the Swiss chemist Albert Hofmann, working on making medicines from lysergic acid, added diethylamide. And he dismissed it as useless, not at all enjoying the "uninterrupted stream of fantastic pictures, extraordinary shapes with intense, kaleidoscopic play of colors" that caused him to leave work early and ride his bike home to lie down. Nineteenth-century physicians called it secale, or just ergot, and it was used kind of like Pitocin is today, to motivate a sluggish uterus into action. It wasn't popular for long, though.

Q: Because it was both a psychotropic drug *and* a deadly poison?

A: Nah. Show me an effective drug of the day that wasn't one or the other. No, it was thought to be too rough on the uterus, causing spasms. And it tended to make the mother throw up, by forcing contractions that were so hard that it "kneaded" (bruised) the cervix. A bruised cervix is an unpleasant thing. The nausea connection was made by a Dr. John Beck, writing in an 1863 edition of *The Retrospect of Medicine* about how you could make women vomit by poking them in the cervix.

Self-experimental test on LSD-25, Albert Hofmann, chemist: "8:00 a.m.—no effect. 8:15—no effect. 8:28.345...I JUST REALIZED I AM GOD AND THE WORLD IS MADE OF SYRUP AND LIGHTNING."

He noted that there were quite a few women on record who vomited every time they had sex, and he figured it was because the penis kept bumping the cervix...which is extremely uncomfortable and an absolute vomit button for some ladies. But to be certain, he started poking cervixes with his finger on his lady patients. And sure enough: "I had a patient myself whom I could make retch at my pleasure by touching the os uteri [cervix] with the tip of the finger, although she could give no explanation herself as to the cause of the retching, or as to why she retched, yet the result of the touch was invariable."

Q: "Make retch at my pleasure..." Wow. Dr. Beck and those penises had something in common. They were both di—

A:—sruptive to the comfort of the patient, most certainly. But that was only one of the reasons ergot lost its popularity. Chloroform was just more reliable.

Q: Okay. Chloroform. How did the kidnapper's drug of choice

John Snow chloroform inhaler of the kind used on Queen Victoria.

become the favored manner of bringing new life into the world?

A: Chloroform *and* ether, both delightful knock-out gases that could be used to anesthetize patients, came into general use around the 1840s. Chloroform was less likely to catch on fire, which is one reason it was preferred by many practitioners. Its beginnings were…rather ignoble. It was first prepared in 1831 by the American chemist Dr. Samuel Guthrie, who combined whiskey with chlorinated lime in an attempt to produce a cheap pesticide.

Then it was found useful in surgeries. Finally the leap was made to childbirth. The beauty of chloroform is described by Mary Ries Melendy in 1903, at a time when using the drug had been standard for around sixty years.

> *The inhalation of chloroform, according to the will of the operator, causes either partial or complete unconsciousness, and, either for a longer or for a shorter time, freedom from pain. In other words, the effects might, with perfect safety, be continued, either for a few minutes, or from time to time, for several hours; indeed, if given in proper cases, and by a judicious doctor, with perfect safety.*

And how did it feel to be put to sleep by gas so as to forgo excruciating pain? Well, let's just say…they should have sent a poet. And, oh! What luck, they did!

Oliver Wendell Holmes was a doctor *and* a poet, talents that came together nicely in a letter he wrote to the first man to publicly demonstrate how ether could be used to put a patient under during an operation. He wrote the American dentist William Morton in 1846 to express his admiration. He told Morton soon the whole world would be speaking of his discovery, so a name ought to be cemented: "The state should, I think, be called anesthesia. This signifies insensibility, more particularly (as used by Linneaus and Cullen) to objects of touch. The adjective will be anesthetic.... The words anti-neuric, aneuric, neuro-leptic, neuro-lepsia, neuro-stasis, seem too anatomical."

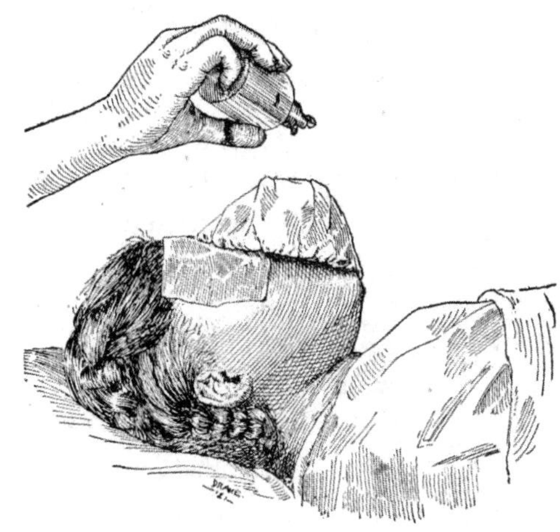

The less exact but more common manner in which women in labor received chloroform.

Q: If chloroform is so great, how come we don't use it now?

A: Oh dear Lord. Because it's *chloroform,* woman! It's not *actually* safe! It turns off the central nervous system, sometimes *all the way* off. It was safe by Victorian standards, standards that included drinking out of the Thames and arming twelve-year-olds with exploding muskets for bear hunting. They didn't have a lot of options back then! Chloroform won out over poisoned ergot, ether (an effective anesthesia with a small history of exploding its patients), or Grandpappy's triple-X rotgut whiskey straight from the jug. But still, it was hard to gauge the right amount of chloroform that would produce a peaceful twilight experience for a delivering mother, and avoid one that would fling her straight into the waiting arms of Jesus before the many natural causes waiting to attack her even got a chance.

Besides, not everyone was convinced of chloroform's safety. Many doctors thought chloroform relaxed the "travailing" body too much, making delivery dangerously slow. And some folks were worried about things that couldn't scientifically actually occur, but you couldn't expect them to know that. In 1863, Dr. Robert Johns of the Royal College of Surgeons in Ireland was published in *The Retrospect of Medicine* giving his theory that inhaling chloroform caused any number of complications, hemorrhage, inflammation, lung problems, and, most terrifyingly, childbed fever.

> *I have known puerperal inflammation frequently to have followed its inhalation, and too often with a fatal result...in the majority of those cases puerperal fever was the cause of death, which...always infectious or otherwise communicable, became epidemicized, after which even those who wisely refused the drug, "charmed it never so sweetly," were thus inadvertently, and, in some instances, hopelessly poisoned.*

As the world was still struggling with the whole "germs" idea, it was easy to mistake the correlation of "the same mothers who partake of chloroform to ease child birth sometimes also, separately, get childbed fever" with the *causation* of "because you're a pitiful excuse for a woman trying to cheat the beautiful pain God gave you with chloroform, it's *giving* you childbed fever."

Q: By the way, what's "childbed fever"? So many fictional characters die of that, but no one ever explains what it actually is.

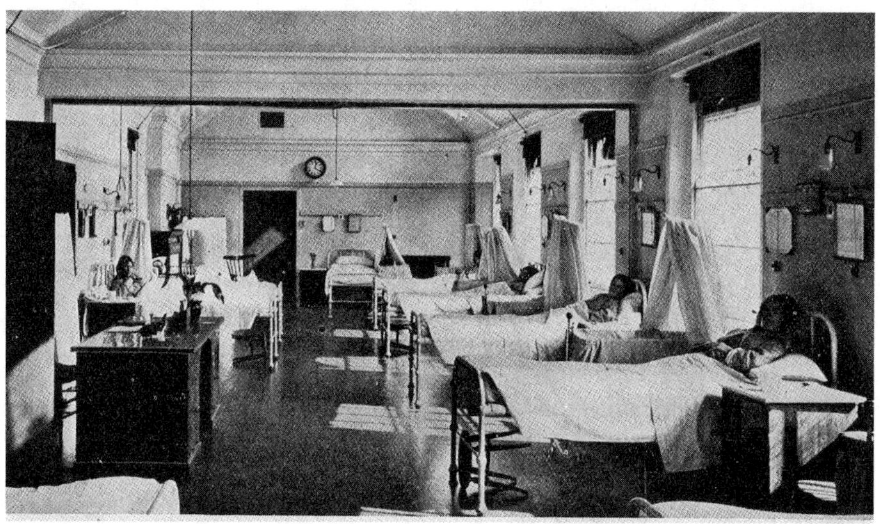

An especially nice "lying-in" hospital.

A: The colloquial for puerperal pyrexia, or puerperal fever. It's a little vague because *puerperal* isn't the name of a virus or bacteria; it just means "related to childbirth." It can be caused by any bacteria that infects the raw and exposed female reproductive tract after birth. With no antibiotics, it was extremely difficult to treat.

And it was often extremely contagious. In a time where no one knew how "contagious" worked. You aren't the first person to be prejudiced against hospitals. In the mid to late 1800s, women in cities were encouraged to go to "lying-in" hospitals to give birth at the hands of a certified physician and be cared for by professional nurses. It was meant to add sanitation and safety to childbirth, and it did in many cases. Except for childbed fever.

It struck the maternity wards in epidemic fashion. Far more often than it did women who were wealthy enough (or poor enough) to deliver their babies at home. A woman would be hale

Of all the famous guys named Holmes in history, only one actually helped solved deadly mysteries.

and hearty with her newborn, but if the woman four beds over took sick with fever, the whole ward might have it within a week.

Q: What was causing it?

A: This would be the time to mention that Victorian doctors didn't wash their hands.

I mean, they would at the end of their examinations...no gentleman is going to go home to his supper after pressing his fingers upon eighteen different bloody cervixes without a spot of freshening up, but there was certainly no reason to wash them *between* patients. You were just going to get them all cervixed up again.

Oliver Wendell Holmes, our poet who gave us our most musical name for knockout gas, actually had an even more pronounced role in making childbirth safer. He wasn't the first or the only doctor to notice that women who got puerperal fever usually shared the same doctor, but he was the best writer. He wrote an essay in the *New England Quarterly Journal of Medicine* in 1843 called "The Contagiousness of Puerperal Fever." What if all these women weren't catching the same disease because they were breathing in the same "bad air," or simply randomly falling to God's design? What if the *doctors* were the ones passing the disease? And...he was largely ignored. He even republished it in the 1850s to more acclaim, but since they still weren't sure *how* the disease spread, the treatise was before its time.

Q: I'm surprised they used all these drugs. Wasn't there some sort of religious outcry against painkillers in delivery? Didn't they think the pain was ordained by God and necessary to the bonding of mother and child?

Eve Cursed by God, *by Marc Chagall.*

A: "Unto the woman he said, I will greatly multiply thy sorrow and thy conception; in sorrow thou shalt bring forth children; and thy desire shall be to thy husband, and he shall rule over thee." —Genesis 3:16

God said, right after Eve ruined paradise for all of us, that her primary punishment would be childbirth, coupled with the unquenchable desire to stay with the man who did the things that caused childbirth. So, yes, as today, many were against the use of painkillers. But not as many as you'd think.

Dr. John H. Dye noticed that God had cursed Adam at the same time to suffer labor and toil for survival. Yet the industrial age of machines had freed Adam's descendants from that curse, and no one thought *that* sinful. So why couldn't it be the same for the Daughters of Eve? "For our part," he said, "we cannot believe the Almighty the cruel, merciless tyrant many picture Him, but believe in His wisdom, mercy and justice. He has placed at our disposal abundant means for our relief if we will but comprehend and apply them."

Dr. Thomas Bullock, writing in an 1896 edition of the periodical *American Practitioner,* counted fear of chloroform and other pain control on religious grounds as one of the many "Obstetrical Superstitions" practitioners like himself must contend with while

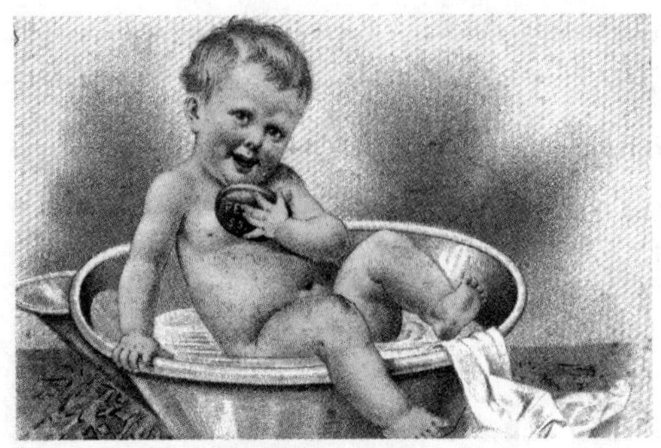

"Good thing I don't walk yet, ladies, cuz the doctor left that cord long enough to trip on."

trying to do his job: "[The patient] will probably demur, saying that Dr. So-and-So told her that if ever under any circumstances she took chloroform it would kill her. If the patient does not object some of the neighboring women will 'chip in,' saying that it is not right to give it; that it is flying in the face of Providence."

He himself believed this ridiculousness on par with the insistence that a woman take tobacco snuff to ease passing the placenta, never raise her arms above her head lest she cause the child to strangle on its umbilical cord, or, my personal favorite: "When the child is born and the doctor is preparing to cut the cord he is sometimes interrupted and told he must cut the cord longer, as the length of the penis at maturity depends on the length the cord is cut."

That last one being an excellent conversation starter with your mother-in-law the next time you have an awkward lull in the conversation. "Say, Linda...when you guys cut Brian's umbilical cord...you cut it awful close, didn't you? I mean, I love the guy, but it was like a two-inch stub, amirite?"

Like many doctors of his time, Bullock used chloroform only in the second stage of labor, when he wished the mother to be semiconscious. Before that he recommended a hearty dose of morphine, to allow her to sleep through the hours of the earliest labor pains.

Q: Knocking a mother out so she can't experience the joy of

childbirth? Awful! How disconnecting and...I'm sorry, they really just *slept* through hours of the feeling that someone was sawing open their lower back with a rusty steak knife?

A: Heh. It's okay. You can admit it. You want morphine and chloroform and ether and ALL the drugs, don't you?

Q: NO! It's dangerous and wrong and...(shhh, okay, no, but seriously, it didn't hurt at all?)

A: We have Queen Victoria's own words, after she gave birth to her eighth child and used chloroform for the first time in 1853. The queen's usually rather dour writing style was ebullient.

> *I have never recovered better, & dearest Albert's untiring, love, tenderness & care for me, have as usual, been my greatest support in my hours of trial. I was taken ill early on the morning on the 7th & a boy was born to great happiness to me. Dr. Snow administered "that blessed Chloroform" & the effect was soothing, quieting & delightful beyond measure.—April 22, 1853*

Q: And the baby suffered no ill effects?

A: Um...none that we can completely blame on the manner of his birth. I mean, all right, it is true that the queen seemed to... downright dislike her youngest son, the first born under chloroform, Prince Leopold.

1858—"...he holds himself as badly as ever and is very ugly, I think uglier than he was..."

1858—"He is tall, but holds himself worse than ever and is a very common looking child, not an engaging face...and not an engaging child."

1859—[Wishing her daughter luck with her own newest baby] "If

Would you rather be disliked by your own mother or by the most powerful woman on earth? Oooh, sorry, Leo, didn't see you there. That's some rotten luck, buddy.

you remember what Leopold was! I hope dear, he won't be like the ugliest and least pleasing member of the whole family."

1859—[Explaining why Leo isn't coming on vacation with the family...he's just too gross] "It would be very troublesome indeed to have him here. He walks shockingly—and is dreadfully awkward—holds himself as badly and his manners are despairing."

1859—"I never cared for you near as much as you do about the baby; I care much more about the younger ones (poor Leopold perhaps excepted)."

She did not describe her other child born with chloroform, Princess Beatrice, in anything but the most glowing terms, so we probably can't blame the painkillers. Though some people did.

The queen's beatdowns of Leopold slowed in her writings after 1859, when she most likely became aware of what was likely the real cause of Leo's trouble: that he was a hemophiliac. At least we *think* she knew. Some historians think Leopold's doctors kept the truth of it from the queen due to the stigma of being a "bleeder." But she knew he was sickly. Since his birth, every bump and tumble that other children wouldn't notice caused internal bleeding, aching joints, and bruising on Leo. Hemophilia (which can be caused by gene mutation but is not necessarily caused by the rampant inbreeding of nineteenth-century European royalty) is carried on the X chromosome, meaning it was Victoria herself who passed the disease to her son, as well as countless of her grandchildren and great-grandchildren.

Q: Forget "Bloody Mary." Slumber parties should involve chanting "Non-Clotting Bloody Victoria" three times into a mirror. Mean queen. What other preparations are needed in the birthing chamber?

A: Not much. It was the desire of all in the medical community that Nature would do most of the work—it was the highest hope of all birth attendants that they wouldn't have to interfere. When labor commenced they mostly kept their hands to themselves if they could, aside from smearing lard on your perineal area, occasional pokes at your vagina to make sure everything was running smoothly, and telling you to be quiet.

Though his wife begged him to change the name, Karl's Sweet Cream No-Sting Vagina Butter remained one of his top sellers.

Q: I'm giving birth, I'm not required to be "quiet." Furthermore… lard on my what now?

A: Lard, oil, or butter was used to keep you from needing episiotomy stitching. A tear like that was much more likely to become infected before antiseptics and antibiotics. So, as Charles H. Robinson's collection of baby advice *The Science of Eugenics and Sex Life* urges, "Pay attention to oiling the vagina and surrounding tissues with pure sweet lard or unsalted butter."

Thank heavens he specifies *un*salted butter. The salted kind would sting something awful.

And as for being quiet, show some dignity. You don't want your doctor thinking he has to deal with *two* crybabies in this birthing. First of all, if you're in a great deal of pain, it's a failing of your own character. One Dr. Dervrees, being quoted in the same publication, says the only reason you have pain at all is because you've corrupted your health through bad choices and sloth: "[Pain] is a perversion of nature caused by living inconsistent with the most healthy conditions of the system, and that such regimen as should insure completely healthy conditions might be counted on with certainty to do away with such pain."

Q: That arrogant little turd! So even in the nineteenth century they expected women to gain only four pounds, survive on kale and prenatal vitamins, and enter the delivery room still sweating from running a triathlon?

A: Mm. Most of those things hadn't been invented—none, if you count eating kale as a modern aberration. But they did expect a supreme display of self-control from the mother during her suffering. And not just men. A young midwife (who had not given birth herself), writing for the same publication, tells the state of the mother she was called upon to deliver of a stillborn child: "The indolent over-fleshy wife of a neighbor sent for me; my parents objected on account of my being so young, but the young husband pleaded that I might come. We...found her one mass of fat lying on the bed weeping and groaning for help." The midwife contrasts that perversion of nature to many other pregnancies she's attended, with healthy women delivering healthy young babes with hardly a yelp.

Q: She's picking on a poor woman whose baby was stillborn for being fat while pregnant?

A: Don't forget "indolent." And whiny. Luckily the Connecticut Training School for Nurses has some tips for helping a laboring mother get through the ordeal with dignity: "The midwife can counsel [the mother] to be brave and not endanger the effect of the pains by useless tossings or loud outcries.... It often helps on a tedious labor if the patient will hold her breath during a pain, and not scream and breathe rapidly, as women are likely to do."

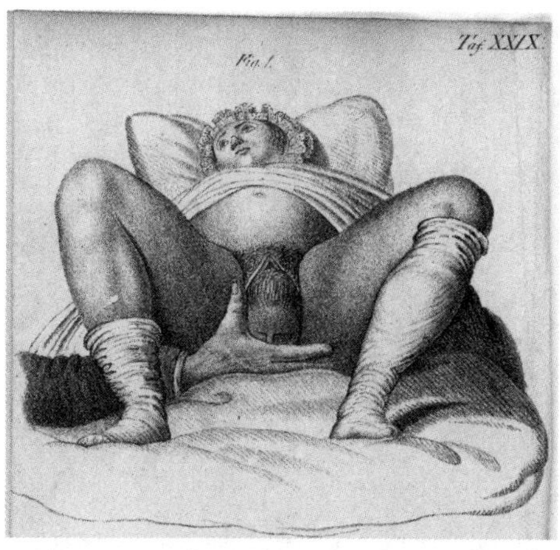

An added benefit of the supine birthing position: Often no pain medication was needed if the water stains on the ceiling were interesting enough.

Q: I fear to ask, but what sort of positions are appropriate for the actual birth?

A: Most doctors encouraged movement and walking until the "grinding" labor pains notched up to "bearing down" pains. As for appropriate positions for childbirth, American and English mothers were trained in two distinct manners for parturition. Americans were to lie on their backs, supine and spread, as is still traditional today.

Englishwomen, according to *The Family Doctor, or The Home Book of Health and Medicine,* written by "A Dispensary Surgeon" in 1858, "should be placed on the bed, previously guarded by some waterproof material on her left side, and not far from the

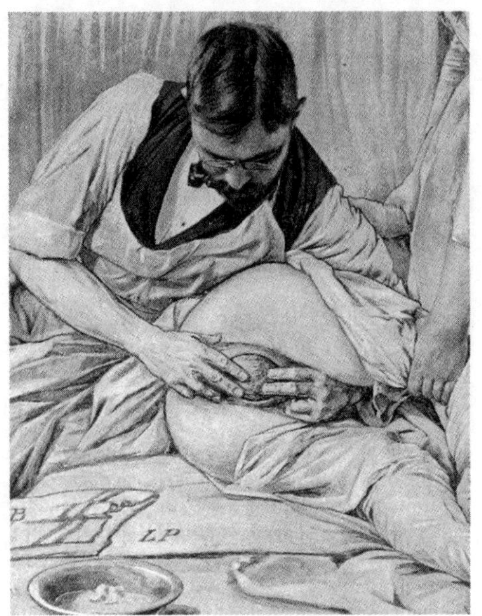
Side delivery as performed by pervert male midwife.

edge, so that needful assistance can be easily rendered. She should have a tightly rolled pillow placed between her knees."

Both of these positions were meant to offer physicians as much access as possible. Other cultures, as depicted in 1883's *Labor Among Primitive Peoples* by George Julius Engelmann, cared more about getting the child to exit the mother than having her vagina accessible, and encouraged the woman to use gravity.

Q: What happens after the birth is over?

A: As little as humanly possible. Bed rest after birth was non-negotiable, clear into the twentieth century. In the infamous *Searchlights on Health* by B. G. Jefferis and J. F. Nichols, the new mother is encouraged to embrace a level of inhuman stillness on par with a Buddhist deity.

> *After the birth of the baby, the mother should be kept perfectly quiet for the first 24 hours and not allowed to talk or see anyone except her nearest relations, however well she may seem. She should not get out of bed for ten days or two weeks, nor sit up in bed for nine days. The more care taken of her at this time, the more rapid will be her recovery when she does get about. She should go up and down stairs slowly, carefully, and as seldom as*

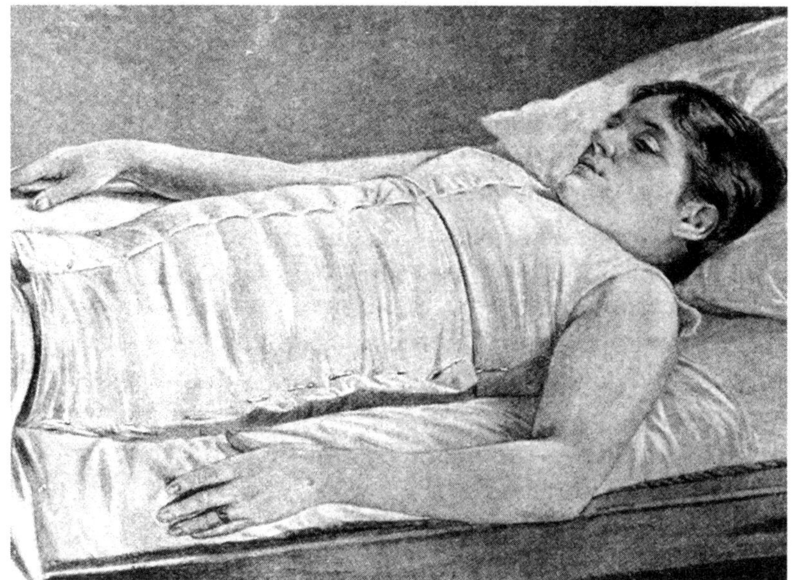

Obstetrical binders were tight cloth wraps intended to help keep a new mother's insides on the inside.

> *possible for six weeks. She should not stand more than is unavoidable during that time, but sit with her feet up and lie down when she has time to rest. She should not work a sewing machine with a treadle for at least six weeks, and avoid any unusual strain or over-exertion.*

It seemed so much could befall a postpartum mother—her organs wrecked and displaced, her strength diminished, fluids trying to regain pre-pregnancy levels—that most doctors seemed to take the stance that if the woman just stayed *still,* very, very still, perhaps her body wouldn't notice the grievous insult it had just suffered.

For rural and working-class women, this would be some of the only "leisure" time their lives would ever allow. It was standard practice for neighbor women and family to dutifully arrive at the recovering mother's home, misplace her crockery, snoop through her correspondences, and gently insult the patient's decorating scheme, all of which helped speed a mother's recovery and reclamation of her own home.

Q: If bed rest was so important, did slaves and servants get time off after having a baby?

A: Oh! Ha-ha! Sure! In fact, the lady of the manor would come down and sponge out their episiotomy tears with heirloom linens thrice daily! HA!

No. Absolutely not. You're ridiculous.

Servants as would be found in upper-class American and British homes would be dismissed from their positions as soon as it was discovered they were with child, even if they were married. Another reason poor women of the era were tempted to conceal pregnancy and another reason doing so was illegal.

As for black American slaves and Native Americans, Victorian science tells us that they didn't *require* bed rest. Or pain control. Or doctors or midwives or...basic human rights. Just a nice dark corner to curl up in for an hour or so. Like a housecat.

John Dye wrote with admiration of the method of birth by Indian "squaws." That is, one that provided no inconveniences to anyone. Giving birth is no reason for supper to be late.

> *A pregnant squaw does not occasion any concern from her companions. She performs the usual drudgery of her life up to the very hour of her labor, making no preparation for the coming "pappoose." When she realizes that the hour for delivery is at hand, she enters her*

cabin or betakes herself to some stream or spring, gives birth, washes the young "Injun" in the cold water, straps it upon her back, and before she has been scarcely missed, has returned a full-fledged mother, and resumes her labors unconscious of having undergone any very wonderful ordeal.

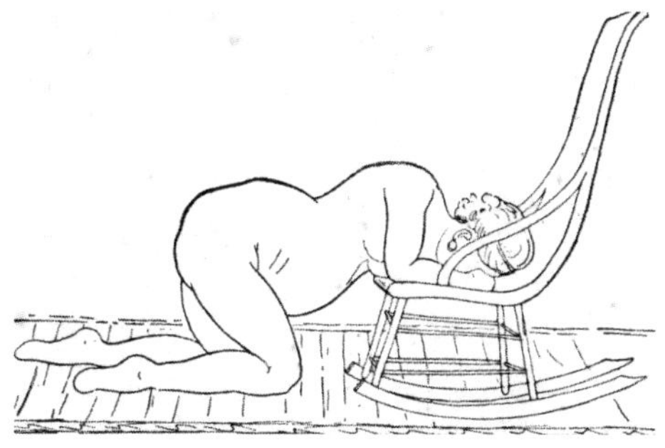

Illustration of the favored birth position of the healthy American Negress.

Q: He honestly believes Native American women just pop out babies (did he say "Injun"?) without even feeling like they've undergone any "ordeal"?

A: Yes. And not just the Injuns, either. African American slaves were also remarkable baby birthers. Hardly slowed the cotton harvest at all. (Least they *better* not slow it.) Says Dye: "It is well known that the Slave women of this country required very little or no attention at confinement. Their labors are generally of short duration, the pain moderate, and the woman is incapacitated from performing her usual avocations only a few hours."

Q: The slave women were expected to be back in the fields picking crops within *hours* of birth, but white women lay in bed for two weeks??

A: I think we're supposed to look at it as...a blessing God bestowed on an otherwise downtrodden people.

Q: Seriously?

A: Believe me, it would be a delight to tell you that I'm joking and men were never this blithe and heartless toward any woman, much less one in labor. But this is what was recorded, on the few occasions it *was* recorded. Welcome to the past. It's quite awful here.

But as in many awful places, food and drink can mitigate the misery. Let's see if that's the case for Victorian children.

4

My Child Will Eat Neither Mush, Mucilage, Porridge, Pablum, Gruel, nor Loblolly. Is Pickiness God's Way of Culling the Herd?

On Feeding Children

Q: Don't bother with an introduction. Just teach me about wholesome old-fashioned eating without making me feel sad or irritated.

A: I am here to serve. Let's learn how to feed our child as healthfully as possible. I'm certain no depressing controversy will be unearthed while pursuing that goal! Now, will you breastfeed or not?

Q: *Seriously?* C'mon. Don't let's argue about breastfeeding versus bottle feeding. It's a very tired argument.

A: I agree. I'm taking it as a given that we both know you're a bad mother if you don't give your Victorian child breast milk. Pathetic excuse for a parent, actually. An utter monster. Murder glinting in your maniacal eye.

Q: How dare you. People like you are why there is so much mother-on-mother hate crime. Or hate-typing, at least, in internet forums. You need to be a little more open-minded about—

A: Oh, calm your engorged teats. You wanted to be Victorian about this, correct? So first consider the availability of scientifically developed FDA and pediatrician-approved baby formula at your local Victorian dry goods store. Nonexistent. There are breast milk substitutes, and I will tell you about them, but to do so will require repeated use of the term "ass milk."

Q: Ass milk…?

A: *I know!* Breastfeeding is less of a lifestyle choice in this world than—especially in the early part of the era—a requirement.

"The Fashionable Mama" excretes maternal love without sacrificing style.

So, when I ask if you will breastfeed, I'm asking whether you will choose to feed the child from your own breast, or enlist the service of a wet nurse. A wet nurse is a woman hired to, depending on your finances, live in your home and nourish the child through its first year, or take your child into her home for the same purpose.

Q: Women gave their babies to strangers for the first year just so they didn't have to nurse? I'll feed my own child, thanks.

A: That was usually considered preferable. Except if you were an unfit milker. According to 1845's *The Maternal Management of Children, in Health and Disease* by Dr. Thomas Bull, there are

"Mothers Who Ought Never Suckle." They include, naturally, a mother who is deathly ill with tuberculosis or any other wasting disease.

But it's not just the sick in *body* who need to find a heartier teat for their babe. Also on the "Do Not Feed" blacklist were nervous or overprotective mothers. Says Bull:

> *The mother who is alarmed at any accidental change she may happen to notice in her infant's countenance,—who is excited and agitated by the ordinary occurrences of the day;—such a parent will do her offspring more harm than good by attempting to suckle it. Her milk will be totally unfit for its nourishment: at one time it will be deficient in quantity,—[and] depraved in its quality.*

Q: If I'm nervous about my newborn's health, like every new mom is...it means that my boobs are depraved and I shouldn't nurse?

A: Oversimplifying, but yes. You suffer from nipple neurosis and you shouldn't inflict it on your infant. So we must find a wet nurse! Physically, you must check to see that her tongue is clean, and digestion good; her teeth and gums sound and perfect; her skin free from eruption, and her breath sweet. As for her breasts, Bull elucidates:

> *A good breast should be firm and well-formed; its size not dependent upon a large quantity of fat, which will generally take away from its firmness, giving it a flabby appearance, but upon its glandular structure, which conveys to the touch a knotted, irregular, and*

hard feel; and the nipple must be perfect, of moderate size, but well developed.

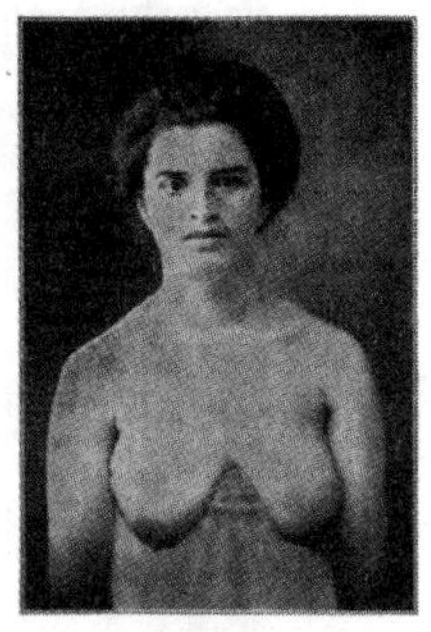

Preferable type of breasts for wet-nursing.

Q: I don't wanna sniff and grope a strange woman.

A: Well, maybe your husband will do it for you. Another important consideration is how your nurse came to be lactating. If she has her own children, she's going to try to feed *them* as well. Not optimal. Rather, seek the rare jewel of the wet nurse, a respectable lactating lady who, in the best case, has recently lost both her husband and baby.

Q: And this newly widowed grieving mother will give better milk than I can because I'm *sooo* nervous that I occasionally get up at night to check that my baby is still sleeping on his back?

A: Put them on their stomach, actually, so they don't choke on spit-up. And so their growing spines aren't compressed. Thoroughly bundled in many blankets so they don't catch a chill. And at any rate, make sure their heads are pointed north. Because of magnetism and air circulation...something. I digress. If the lactating woman is going to be all woe-is-me because of recent misfortunes, then no, don't employ her.

To illustrate the damage of a fretful wet nurse, Dr. Bull tells of being called to tend a baby in convulsions. He was puzzled, because he'd seen the baby just a few days before, healthy and suckling happily with his nurse.

The story came out that the wet nurse's father had paid the girl a call, screamed at her, and beat her.

Strict orders were given to forbid the man the house in future: but the mischief was done; for it was but too

The trick with canned milk is to find that perfect balance of botulism: a little zing with minimal fatalities.

> *evident that the alarming state in which I found the child had been produced by the deleterious change which had taken place in the nurse's milk. Remedial measures were used; the breast-milk withheld; and the infant, although it continued for many days in a doubtful state, eventually recovered; the young woman's milk, however, was altogether driven away, and another wet-nurse was, without delay, obliged to be obtained.*

Q: That's horrible. Every single thing you just said was horrible. No wet nurse. What other options were there?

A: Toward the end of the century the process for making "evaporated" or "condensed" milk would become widespread, allowing many "milk food" substitutes to hit the market. There were problems, of course. The canning process was not yet reliable, the primitive baby bottles and pap boats were difficult to clean, and lack of refrigeration caused rampant sickness in infants, particularly in summer months when spoilage was higher. Which is another reason so many mothers reached for ass milk.

French nurses holding newborns to suckle directly from donkey udders, 1895.

Q: . . .

A: Mm? What? Do you have a question?

Q: I swear you're enjoying this horror show. Do you mean donkey milk? Can you just call it that?

A: Historical accuracy is my most sincere goal; they legitimately called it ass m—

Q: I'm closing the book.

A: FINE! Fine, yes, donkey. How we all agreed that *cows*—those foul, dead-eyed, flea-bitten fecal bags of flatulence—were the animal it was okay to drink fluids out of is a wonderment. The milk of the donkey, though it has fallen out of fashion, has been a favorite health drink since the time of the ancient Greeks. Samuel Barker recommended it heartily in 1860's *Children and How to Manage Them in Health and Sickness:*

> *Asses' Milk, in recovery from illness, when the vital powers continue very low, has, with the addition of cream, occasionally answered where all other food has signally failed. This is probably due to its containing*

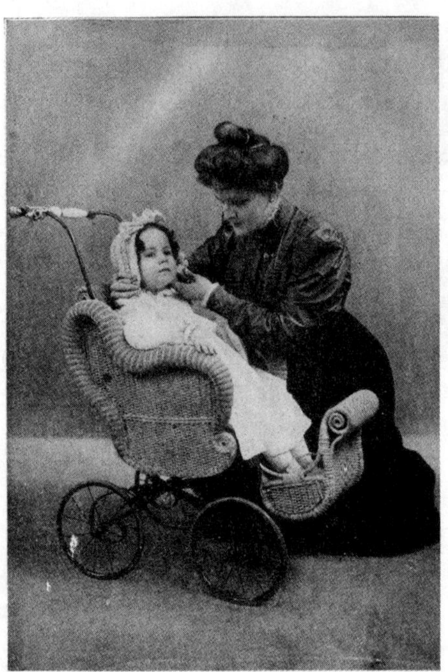

"No, thank you. I'm watching my teeny figure. Trying to keep it alive."

so small a proportion of casein,—the indigestible element. Unfortunately this milk is not readily procured except in large towns.

It doesn't pack the all-around punch of cow's milk, which, whether by nature or selective breeding, has the most protein of domesticated animal milk, including human. But that's a good thing where babies are concerned. Donkey milk has more lactose (sugar), and is most similar to human milk, being gentle on tiny tummies and quite sweet.

At any rate, within a few months you can wean your child to pap, a watered- or milked-down version of whatever cooked cereal grain your family regularly eats.

Q: Once they start eating solid food, how much should I give them?

A: However much they ask for. For the love of all that's holy, don't follow any rules about portion except the ones set forth by your own baby. As you'll see, horrible results await if you—

Q: But we said…we said we weren't going to do horrible for a while!

A: Oh, pet, I know. It's the fault of neither of us that the answer to nearly every question you ask about a Victorian child's well-being leads to tragedy. Now buck up, because here we go.

A young doctor, who had recently become a father, told of the alarm he felt as he observed his nurse—the same beloved old lady who raised him from infancy—feeding his newborn child.

"Seriously, Ma, no matter how much I fuss, cut me off at six ounces. And if I'm wobbly, take my keys, too."

> *Then, the pap she made for the infant, thick enough for the spoon to stand upright in, was to be forced into the tiny stomach, to prevent the wind getting in; and when it had been introduced in such unmerciful quantities as necessarily to occasion a degree of distention so uneasy as to throw the poor child almost into convulsions, more fuel was to be added to the flame because it was a case proved in her own mind, that wind had got in nevertheless, and that the child could cry for nothing but wind, and wind could come from nothing but emptiness; so that the more she kept stuffing, the more the child cried, and the more the child cried, the more she kept stuffing it.*

The doctor interceded, respectfully, to stop his dear nursemaid's good-hearted attempts to kill his child. When he tried to educate her about new ideas of what infants and small children should eat, she responded with great hostility.

> *"Don't tell me, my dear young gentleman, of your halves, and your thirds, and your narrow stomachs, and small vessels; how should you men know anything about it? Didn't I bring up you and your sister, and should have brought up all the whole eleven your mamma had, had they not turned out so sickly and fitty, that there was no rearing them any how."*
>
> *She spoke truly enough, for by all accounts, we were all sickly and fitty, and I verily believe, nothing but a very accidental strength of stomach, in the case of my sister and myself, prevented our going the way of the other nine; that is, being killed with kindness; stuffed, and crammed, and coddled out of this wicked world, almost as soon as we were born into it.*

Q: Did you just tell me about the death of nine babies in the form of a folksy anecdote?

A: No...I just related it. There often appeared a very black humor in medical literature regarding infant mortality. When people have to cope with the un-copable, sometimes "whistling by the graveyard" humor is a comfort.

At any rate, a small child tends to eat only as much as they need, especially when their dietary options are so dull. If you follow the aforesaid rules, and remember never to force more on the child than needed, your child will thrive. Or at least survive. Maybe. Other foods were considered dangerous to children as well.

Q: It sounds like *all* the foods were dangerous.

A: Yes, but some were particularly depraved. Mostly the ones associated with happiness, unfortunately.

According to George Henry Rohe in 1890's *Text-Book of*

The last known picture of "Tinks" and "Cubby" Smythe, the notorious Pickle Thugs, before their nationwide crime spree ended in a four-day standoff with law enforcement.

Hygiene, the "digestive derangements of children" include "nuts, candies, pies, fruit-cakes, and, above all, pickles."

Tasty foods are usually spiced. Spices, like nuts, are harvested in balmy pagan lands full of passion and partial nudity. Pickling (a much more common form of food preservation in centuries past) requires spices, as well as vinegar. Vinegar is nothing more than demon-alcohol gone putrid with a bacterial infection. These foods were thought to lead children, particularly girls, to behave erratically. Yet so many mothers were ignorant that they were sending their children down the path of Perdition on a dinner plate.

Says Newton Riddell, the author of 1902's *Child Culture According to the Laws of Physiological Psychology and Mental Suggestion,* "The appetite for strong drink is often the result of the use of condiments, pastry, tea, coffee and tobacco. These things do not feed, but stimulate. They do not strengthen, but irritate. They set the appetite and passions on fire, thereby creating a demand for stronger stimulants.... Thousands of children have gone down into vice and crime propelled by appetites perverted by unwholesome food prepared by mother's hand." The deceivingly decent

Thurbers' Fruit Preserves doesn't even try to pretend your children won't be driven to fevered brutality by its product.

foods that will ruin your child are legion. Barker says "The flesh of immature animals—veal, lamb, &c—is unfit for children; so are all rich, coarse, indigestible things, as pork, goose, duck, fat and salted meats, which often give rise to sickness, spasm, looseness of the bowels, skin diseases, &c. Rich cakes, pastry, new or heavy bread, and sweetmeats [fruits and nuts preserved with sugar], are objectionable."

Barker recommends children be given vegetables to stave off rickets, but only when boiled and salted to prevent worms. And he is particular about the vegetables, reminding the parent that "old, mealy potatoes, well-cooked, carefully washed, and free from lumps, are preferable to new."

Fruit is also suspect. Barker warns us that "apricots, peaches, plums, damsons, cherries, &c, should, as a rule, be withheld."

Louisa Caroline Tuthill, author of 1885's *Joy and Care, a Friendly Book for Young Mothers,* agrees: "The indulgence in fruit of any kind should be limited while children are young," she says. But the absolute worst (and this goes out to every modern parent who includes dried apricots from the bulk bins at the warehouse store in their child's lunchbox as "dessert") is the deadly influence of dried fruit.

> *Dried fruits can seldom be eaten with safety. Raisins are extremely indigestible; there is no stomach, unless it be that of the ostrich, that can master the skin of a raisin: we have known three instances of convulsions and death from the excessive use of this fruit. Dried cherries, apples and peaches, are altogether unfit to be received into the stomachs of children. Even the fig and the prune cannot be freely indulged in with entire safety.*

Q: Fruit is bad? That can't be...Weren't figs and pomegranates and quince eaten all the time in the Bible? It seems like God is pro-fruit.

A: Don't presume to know God's stance on produce; it's extremely arrogant. Mixing arrogant women, fruit, and God all into one story is what damned mankind to this kind of suffering and toil in the first place.

Q: What *shall* my child eat, then?

A: Here's a good guideline. Before you feed your child anything, ask yourself: Is it a nice dried bread or cereal paste? If not, has it been boiled until it resembles a pot of wet washrags? Neither? Then it's best for the child to avoid it.

Says Barker, "Throughout childhood none but the plainest food should be given." Riddell elaborates that eating meat would inflame a child to evil. He points out that carnivorous beasts fed only vegetarian diets become docile. Which, granted, was likely due to severe protein deficiency slowing starving them to death. He suggests any child of an animal-like nature also be denied meat: "The child of a vicious or cruel nature should not be allowed any meat during its growing period; while those of a tame disposition, and especially the timid and diffident, may use meat once a day with good results. No doubt humanity would be much better off morally and spiritually, if all abstained from the use of meats."

Q: Does it help with the child's morality and spirit if I make an effort to give him only organic food?

A: Have...have you been feeding him *inorganic* food? Because if you have been—say, porridge made from metal shavings and feldspar chippings, say—I highly recommend you stop and, yes, go "organic."

Q: Don't be snippy. It's an honest question.

A: I'm snippy because "organic" is an ill-used word that very few consumers even understand today. But if you are wanting to emulate Victorians, by all means feed your child from the overpriced, puny, and quickly rotting food aisle. In the Victorian era most food would have technically been grown "organically," though without a Food and Drug Administration, much of it was adulterated afterward. Still, modern pesticides or preservatives would have been absent. Just be sure, if you do decide to go organic, to pay attention to our chapter devoted to keeping a child healthy. Pesticides exist for a reason. That reason is anal worms.

Q: My child won't eat this way! And I don't really blame him. How do I persuade him to accept such a bland diet?

A: There are many ways to direct a child toward the healthful eating of repugnant food. Mrs. Tuthill favors exposure therapy, introducing the food to the child in much the same way one would gently lead an arachnophobe to accept that they will spend the rest of their lives locked in the dank cellar where only the hundreds of spiders they share their space with will hear their screams.

Waywardness should not be yielded to. Let the eye of the child become familiarized to the food, and it will

gradually lose its annoying power. The next step is to accustom the nose to bear its effluvium without repugnance: the stomach is much influenced by the eye and the nose. The taste is next to be reconciled. This is best done at a time when the child is strongly tempted to eat, by hunger.

Tuthill's language choice says a lot about the food of the day. "Annoying, effluvium, repugnance, reconciled." She knows it's gross. Just like we all know strained pees, tofu spinach scrambles, and eggplant casseroles are disgusting to a child. But it turns out good-tasting food is for sinners. So what are you going to do? Give the child all the nuts and pickles he wants and then spend the rest of your life scheduling activities around his parole hearings?

The nineteenth century was very in touch with the difficulties children faced, and frequently tried to address them in children's literature. Take the story "Augustus Who Would Not Have Any Soup," again from the brilliant Heinrich Hoffmann's *Struwwelpeter* storybook.

> *The third day comes. O what a sin!*
> *To make himself so pale and thin.*
> *Yet, when the soup is put on table,*
> *He screams, as loud as he is able*
> *"Not any soup for me, I say!*
> *O take the nasty soup away!*
> *I won't have any soup to-day!"*
> *Look at him, now the fourth day's come!*
> *He scarce outweighs a sugar-plum;*
> *He's like a little bit of thread;*
> *And on the fifth day he was—dead.*

And...that's pretty much that. A theme we will revisit often in this book: There is no kindness in mollycoddling a child. Eat your soup or we'll be using it to adorn your tiny grave.

A child's pickiness when presented with the few foods that were both plentiful before the era of mass agriculture *and* non-deranging

"You can come out when you've finished your soup, Gus."

might be one of the reasons Victorian health advocates put emphasis on health-improving *beverages*. It may be awful. But at least in liquid form it slides down faster. Of course, choosing the right beverage for your child is in itself a minefield.

Q: What shall my child drink? Besides the donkey...*stuff* you keep bringing up.

A: First, it's a mistake to let your child just have a drink whenever they're thirsty. It leads to drinking. Which makes sense. But drinking, see, in turn leads to *drinking,* as in grown-up booze guzzling.

Take it from Dame Henrietta Barnett in 1894's *The Making of the Body:*

> *Some people are always wanting "something to drink," and these like to take liquid in some form, not only at meals, but at all hours. This is not a good habit, and one that should not be encouraged; for at first children only ask for water, but in later life they want beer, and too easily turn into the public-houses for a drink, to the ruin of their own health and the destruction of the happiness of those who love them or depend upon them.*

So proceed with caution, and most certainly avoid "soft-drinks" (nonalcoholic but still festive in nature, like lemonade, sarsaparilla, or fresh fruit punch), which teach a child to associate pleasure with hydration. Because before you know it, they'll be dancing for pennies while gunslingers fire pistols at their feet just so they can afford a single shot a of gasoline-grade whiskey. As Barker warns:

> *The great danger of engendering in childhood, a habit that may culminate in the drunkard of after years, is too serious and imminent to be passed over. Who can say that the mere taste of wine or spirits with which a child is ceremoniously indulged on occasions as a "harmless luxury" shall not beget a fondness, that growing with his or her growth, will develop into the insatiable craving that inevitably makes the hopeless, loathsome sot?*

A healthy child needs only clean water and fresh milk. An *under*weight child, however, must be plied with many fortifying and horrific "beverages." One of the most popular drinks for thin or sickly children was "toast-water." And if you're picturing that time you tripped over the dog and dropped a slice of bread in her water bowl, where it dissolved into something more disgusting than anything she's ever left in a tightly coiled pile on your lawn, you're on the right track!

Toast-water is simple and health-restorative, and Barker gives us an easy recipe.

> *Toast thoroughly, but not to a cinder, half a slice of a loaf, of the usual size and of a day or two old, put it into a jug, and pour over it a quart of water which has been boiled and cooled; and, after two hours, pour off the water gently from the bread. A small piece of orange or of lemon-peel, put into the jug at the same time as the bread, is a great improvement to toast-water.*

For Barker, the beauty of toast is that it brings taste (as it was defined by nineteenth-century standards) and color to water without affecting its purity (which it seldom contained anyway). He did not consider that this particular flavor burst of soggy bread may not have been as enticing as hoped. But it was worth it if it brought down fever: "Toast-water may be used at will in every febrile affection. It diminishes the heat of the mouth, the throat, and the stomach; and, by sympathy, that of the whole body."

Well, that's not how fevers work, and wet toast is not generally considered an antipyretic (fever reducer). But I imagine there were many times just the mention of toast-water was enough to give children the chills.

If your child is very young, or very ill, it's best to skip the toast-water and go straight to the ass milk I mentioned above. Ass milk is the unchallenged champion of restorative drafts.

Q: STOP saying...Ugh! Just...are there any fortifying beverages I might give my child that involve neither soggy toast nor squeezing *any* animal's nipples?

A: That high-and-mighty "I'm too good to milk a donkey" attitude will infect your child as surely as disease, madam. Nonetheless, you are in luck. There are many forgotten beverages of the nineteenth century that offer health benefits to children and adults.

- **Apple Tea**—This is not apple juice or cider, both of which contain too much sugar and have been known to lead to sexual curiosity. Rather, apple tea is made by pouring boiling water over sliced apples, cooling the water, and then giving the child the not noticeably altered water and telling them how fortunate they are that it doesn't have toast in it.
- **Orgeat**—Today orgeat is used as a drink mixer. In the Victorian era it had more important applications. "Blanch

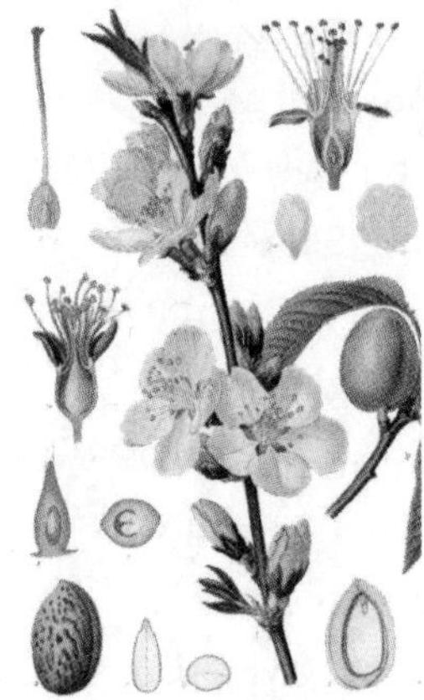

Botanical drawing of the sweet almond tree. Which looks just like the deadly bitter almond tree. So choose wisely, and may the odds be ever in your favor.

two ounces of sweet almonds, and four bitter almonds. Beat to a paste, and rub into milky water. Is a good treatment for upset stomach and heartburn, though some children might develop a strong rash from use."

There may or may not be a connection between the rash mentioned in that recipe and the one often caused by prussic acid, or as we in the twenty-first century call it, cyanide, which is contained in bitter almonds. Bitter almonds grow wild, look extremely similar to the common "sweet" almond, yet contain fifty times more cyanide. Depending on the concentration of cyanide in the nuts, the size of the person eating them, and how fast they are ingested, even a small handful can be instantly fatal. So, yeah, be careful with that.

- **Mustard-whey**—Take half an ounce of bruised mustard seeds and one pint of milk and boil them together until the milk is curdled.

  Drinking the nonlumpy bits of your mustard milk is thought to help ease dropsy by stimulating your kidneys to help you pee. However, it might be wise to remember that today we call dropsy "edema" and it can signify severe organ failure. So if the mustard doesn't work, off you go to the emergency room, okay?

- **Rennet-whey**—"Infuse a moderate-sized piece of rennet [scrapings from inside a cow's stomach] in a sufficient quantity of boiling water...stir a table-spoonful of it into three pints of milk; cover up the mixture with a clean cloth, and place it before the fire until it forms a uniform curd."

Then squeeze the curd until the juice (whey) comes out. What you end up with is basically...very fresh cheese-water. It will help a child with their...Pshh. Between you and me, it'll help them never again complain of whatever ailment made you force cheese juice down their throats.

Marsh-mallow Tea—Oh, now *here* we have something delightful-sounding that the little ones might actually...Wait. No. I'm sorry.

Before marshmallows were mass-produced sugar puff-balls, they were just the dirty, cancerous-looking dried root of the *Althaea officinalis* plant: thick, tough, and fibrous. Eventually French chefs would make a nice meringue sweet that may or may not have had *Althaea* root extract, and the marshmallow as it *should* be would be born. Until then, you're stuck with the old marsh-mallows, which, when boiled, make a tea that helps keep the kidneys from "gravelling" (producing kidney stones).

The marsh-mallow. Complete with its own roasting stick.

Q: I just realized we've not yet touched on drunk babies in this chapter, even though we're discussing drinks. Are we done with drunk babies?

A: No. And if I can't say "ass milk,"

you can't keep referring to "drunk babies." Just because a parent administers medicinal alcohol to her child doesn't mean "drunk babies." In fact, your job as a parent is to control the child's consumption, giving the child just enough liquor to ease their suffering without making a drunkard out of them. You can see how easily a child might fall to drunkenness, considering what their other beverage options are. It is a dangerous balance a parent must master.

Q: But they can suckle donkeys, and have all the cow-gut drippings and cyanide they want?

A: Correct. I can guarantee you *those* beverages will never be over-indulged in. And perhaps a little cyanide builds character? Have you considered that? Character so desperately lacking in today's youth?

Q: When *is* it appropriate to give my child alcohol, and what kind shall they drink?

A: As we have seen, Barker is violently against instilling alcoholism in children through the use of it in medication. He is right to be wary; whiskey was the secret ingredient in so many patent medicines. But even he allows some instances where alcoholic beverages can improve a child's health. Such as the following:

By the age of ten, children should be able to discern a good sherry. For medicinal use, naturally.

- **Measles:** "Wine and water, or weak brandy and water, should be given at intervals, to rally the flagging powers."
- **Poor appetite:** "Pure, light, properly-brewed, honest, well hopped beer, which—a wineglassful or so—in cases of flagging appetite, may be sipped during dinner, and so taken, will create a zest for food that would probably not otherwise be cared for."
- **Glandular enlargement** (the doctor does not specify which glands respond best to this treatment, so we may assume it applies to all of them, from prostate to pancreas to pituitary): Mix "five to ten grains of chlorate of potash, or the same of carbonate of soda in a wine-glassful of beer or milk, three times a day."
- **Common cold:** "Gargle often with tepid port wine."
- **Fainting spells:** "Half-a-glass or so of genuine port wine, with a dry unsweetened biscuit twice or thrice a day, as for luncheon, and again an hour before tea, is often useful; a wineglassful of light, mild, pure bitter ale should also be sipped during dinner."
- **Rickets:** "A teaspoonful of steel wine [wine that had been mineral-fortified by soaking pieces of steel in it for a few weeks] three times daily, and double this quantity of freshly-made lime-water."
- **In cases of extreme illness:** "Strong beef-tea, wine, brandy, cream, the contents of an egg, can be so administered, and life thus sustained."

Q: So...only give a child alcohol if...you've got a child and some alcohol.

"DANCE, RUMMY!"

A: Medical options were fewer then, you know. *Any* substance that produced a nondeadly effect could be considered medicine. Which is why Barker also recommended various internal uses of alcohol for ringworm, epilepsy, scarlet fever, whooping cough, and straining while pooping.

Q: What if my child rejects alcoholism and instead copes with the discomforts of life by eating too much? Is this a problem?

A: Rarely, in this century. Obesity was not the scourge of childhood back then like it is today. Food wasn't as easily available, and when it was, it was usually gross. An obese child was rare, sometimes to the point of being carnival-worthy. And there were many of the opinion that a fat child was a happy child. Like Pye Henry Chavasse, who in his 1872 compilation of rants about the trouble with kids these days, *Aphorisms on the Mental Culture and Training of a Child,* explains,

Ruby Westwood and her brother Wilfred were known as the New Zealand Giants, and toured with their family as medical curiosities (weight, 242 pounds at age thirteen).

> *Why fat children are jolly—the reason being that laughing is good for the digestion; hence people who laugh become fat; while, on the other hand, grieving is bad for the digestion; hence persons who grieve become thin. A laughing child is usually a fat child, while a cross child is generally a thin child—such [a] one as the latter is said to cry all the flesh off his bones!*

But Chavasse is speaking of a charming plumpness. *Gluttony*

That hair is begging to be pulled. Laura was asking for it, flaunting her curls like that. Tsk-tsk.

is a sin no matter what the century. In 1854's *Flowers for Children,* Lydia Maria Francis Child tells the story of Little Laura: "If her brother comes and pulls one of her curls, just for fun, she stamps her foot, and says, 'Get away, Tom.' This is because she has eaten too much."

And here we see the true danger: overeating lowers a girl's tolerance for having her hair yanked. Gawd, Laura. Can't you take a joke? If you didn't want your curls sproinged, maybe you shouldn't let them bounce around for anyone to grab?

Laura isn't the only storybook glutton suffering for her lack of self-control. Witness Mary the Little Glutton from Dr. Henry (Heinrich) Hoffmann's *Slovenly Betsy* storybook. She was always stuffing her face with food. Then one day she had to contend with those who desired sweets even more than she did.

Bees try to eat her sweet face. That's called "irony," Mary.

Q: So...for a healthy child, feed them bland overcooked starches, lots of booze, a sprinkling of poisons, and no frenzy-inducing fruit. That about right?

A: And ass m—

Q: Yes, of course. And ass milk.

A: This is a safe dietary outline for nineteenth-century children, yes. Partly because Victorians were suspicious of anything

With fright she shrieks, and tries to run,
But ah! 'tis all in vain;
Upon her light the angry bees,
And make her writhe with pain.

that caused primal pleasure, like sugary or spicy food. But mostly for practical reasons. Preservation was unreliable, spoilage a given, farming methods temperamental, vermin and bacteria abundant. These constraints made many of the healthy foods of today unavailable or unpredictably dangerous. Inexpensive plain foods, inadvertently made safe through alcohol or boiling, were the smartest choices to feed a child. And if they didn't like it, well, in the next chapter we explore ways of dealing with a truculent child.

5
A Study of Technique Regarding Spanking, Birching, Caning, and Whipping
A Complete Guide to Disciplining Your Child

"Stop this at once, you heartless cow!
I say, does the queen know of this injustice?"

Children enter this world evil. It's all they know. They have no concept of right or wrong, and their selfishness is boundless, making all babies, in practice, sociopaths.

Q: You're a big hit at Mommy and Me playgroups, aren't you?

A: I would have been in the Victorian age! When it was common knowledge that your child is imbued with what religious leaders call Original Sin. And it's your job as a parent to tidy up the moral mess you gave birth to. This means discipline. Punishment, guidance, restriction, punishment, heartfelt talks, life lessons, and punishment. Administer these steadfastly, and your child will not only grow a soul, but become a strong and pious bastion of self-control and laudable table manners.

Q: I don't believe in "Original Sin." Babies are born innocent. Are baby birds sinners because they selfishly chirp for food when they're hatched?

A: Birds have no souls. That's why we eat them. John Wesley, a founder of the Methodist Church, wrote sermons studied even today to illustrate the inherent wickedness of children, citing not only Scripture but how you can tell just by *looking* at the little weasels.

In his highly influential sermon "The Doctrine of Original Sin," Wesley reminds parents, "[The sins of babies] begin when they first show wrong tempers: such as plain, undeniable forwardness, revenge, self-will, which is as soon as they have any exercise of reason."

You know you've seen this. The face that reddens and crinkles in rage at the broccoli you set on his high chair tray. He doesn't care about the effort you made, surrounding the organic steamed vegetables with tiny plastic hippos and giraffes, giving unique voices and personality foibles to each toy, then creating an entire storyboarded adventure in which they (and your child) eat the invading tree aliens and save Planet Applesauce.

In Adam's Fall
We finned all.

Thy Life to mend,
This Book attend.

"The Alphabet," from The New England Primer, *one of America's earliest schoolbooks, gets straight to the point. ("In Adam's fall we sinned all...")*

You will get no appreciation, Mother, for this child knows neither gratitude nor benevolence. He will throw the fruits *and* veggies of your labor down to join the matted filth of your carpet, and he will *maintain direct eye contact with you* while he does it. That little hobgoblin knows *precisely* what he's doing.

Today it's broccoli he's smashing into the ground. Unless he is disciplined firmly, tomorrow it will be the faces of children taking too long at the water fountain. Until one day the only recipients of his defiance will be the prison guards escorting him in and out of the courtroom.

Q: Wait. I know this one. If we're getting biblical, it's "spare the rod, spoil the child," right?

A: Absolutely. We learn this from the anonymous "A Mother," who wrote *A Few Suggestions to Mothers on the Management of Their Children* in 1884. First, the Bible makes it clear that beating kids with a stick is essential to a healthy childhood.

"In the Bible," she writes, "the proper correction of children is not only mentioned, but is even insisted upon as one of the duties of parents to their children."

The proof is recorded in the Book of Proverbs:

> *Foolishness is bound in the heart of a child; but the rod of correction shall drive it far from him.*
>
> *Withhold not correction from the child; for if thou beatest him with the rod, he shall not die. Thou shalt beat him with the rod, and shalt deliver his soul from hell.*

Q: So...I am to...beat the love of Jesus into my child?

A: Jesus only ever beat money-changers, and they had it coming. He was notably gentle with children, even advising grown-ups to act more like them. No, biblical child-discipline advice tends to come to us from the Old Testament, specifically the proverbs of King Solomon. Back then God was a great deal more...smitey.

There were a few fringe arguments, bordering on blasphemy, against the biblical edict of corporal punishment in Victorian times, like that which comes to us from a 1900 edition of the periodical *Humane Review.* The writer, Honnor Morten, who was not only a woman, but unmarried and childless—and a *smoker*—opened her article with a quote from the godless Nietzsche. So, we take her observations as we would those of any mildly deranged person with a frustrated uterus and disgusting personal habits. Also, she indulged that smarmy penchant some people have of reading the *rest* of our favorite childhood Bible stories, like a killjoy Paul Harvey.

She points out that though the "spare the rod" decree *is* in the Bible, and made by the wise King Solomon, "Solomon's sons were

Jesus knew a thing or two about comforting children with strict parents.

not such a success that we should strive to bring up our children on his methods if we thought about it at all. Besides, Solomon says we are to beat our servants till their sides bleed: we have given over beating our servants—is it not about time we gave over beating our sons?" I would like to mention that it's probably not coincidence that as beating servants became unpopular, the refrain of "It's so hard to find good help!" rose among the gentry.

Furthermore, there is no way to tell what sort of men Solomon's sons became. He had by most accounts seven hundred wives and a spare three hundred concubines. But the author was likely referring to the son who succeeded Solomon as king of Israel, Rehoboam.

Rehoboam certainly believed in tough love. And yes, his reign was rather troubled. His subjects asked him for kinder treatment than they'd suffered under Solomon. Rehoboam, who'd been raised and likely liberally beaten by the wisest man in history, told the people of Israel that he would be even *crueler* than his father.

He declared, "My little finger shall be thicker than my father's loins. And now whereas my father did lade you with a heavy yoke, I will add to your yoke: my father hath chastised you with whips, but I will chastise you with scorpions."

Rehoboam invites his subjects to suck his mighty pinky and eat scorpions if they don't like the harsh way his father taught him to rule.

Q: "My little finger is thicker than my father's lo—?"

A: There are many ways to interpret that line. Hips. Probably meant hips. Doesn't matter. The point is, Rehoboam wasn't a terribly successful king. People started worshipping random gods instead of the one he told them to, there were enough wandering cults of male prostitutes to warrant mention, then some civil war...It wasn't a terribly successful reign.

Q: Sounds like "spare the rod and scorpions, save your entire kingdom."

A: No, it sounds like one particular son made God mad by bragging about his Power Pinky and suffered duly.

Q: Okay. Despite this, most experts thought beating was the right approach to child discipline?

A: First, I've never met anyone who *didn't* consider themselves an expert on childcare.

Second, yes, even the most gentle-minded of those who wrote

books on how to raise up children believed in corporal punishment, though they wanted it done with control and compassion.

In 1835's *The Father's Book, or Suggestions for the Government and Instruction of Young Children, on Principles Appropriate to a Christian Country,* Theodore Dwight advocates practicing "safe" forms of child-beating. If you beat a child all the time, Dwight warns, you will "deaden those feelings which should be fostered." The punishment itself "should produce short but real pain," and certain weapons and targeted areas of the body are preferable. "A blow with the hand upon a child's head," for example, "may stupefy without stinging and may produce lasting injury. The bones are tender and small, and a light rod is safer than the hand."

"A Mother" agrees that head-shots are ill-advised but feels the era's popular "thwack on the hand with a ruler" wasn't much better.

"The habit of giving a child a slap and a shake for a fault is not only injudicious," she tells us, "but is seldom attended with a good result. Boxing children's ears and striking the hands hard are also unwise punishments, and are sometimes attended with unlooked-for and even serious consequences. The ears especially, being a delicate part of the body, should not be struck."

Rather, "Mother" directs us to Nature's Own Naughty Seat, roundly padded with cushion and holding none of those tiny bones that seem so eager to snap. She even weighs in on the most pleasant spanking accoutrement: "The good old-fashioned punishment of a good flagellation with a thin, soft, old leather, or carpet slipper, not with the sole of the slipper, however, is still the best mode of punishment where severe correction is found necessary, for besides not

"I told you, you're not allowed to eat raisins! They anger up the blood and make you violent!"

harming in the least it is yet a punishment most generally disliked by children, and it has invariably a salutary effect."

Q: Nobody could think of an effective, less violent way to punish a child?

A: In *Self-Culture, and Perfection of Character, Including the Management of Youth,* Orson Squire Fowler tells the story of a friend's willful and disobedient five-year-old daughter. Her father had tried everything to quell her fits and bring her under control. "He had used the rod, and tried coaxing, but all to no purpose," Fowler writes. "Nothing he could do had yet subdued her. She would break out into most violent fits of anger, throw herself on the floor, beat her head against it, strike, kick, and exhibit the utmost fury."

So, this exasperated father tried a new technique, one that he had learned from his brother, the less published but just as vocal Lorenzo Niles Fowler: "The next morning, on his daughter having one of her mad fits, he poured a pitcher of water on her head."

Nothing happened the first time, but by the fifth pitcher, the girl calmed down and did as she was told. This technique worked, explained Fowler, because of "the sudden shock it gives the whole system, especially when poured on the top of the head, where the great pole or center of sensation is located." Plus at some point it probably feels a bit like drowning.

Q: Is that...that sounds like the concept behind waterboarding.

A: Oh, no! No, no, no! Nothing so horrid! Especially not compared to the origin of this method, which was Lorenzo and Orson's father repeatedly dunking Lorenzo's head in a full water barrel to break his spirit. *That's* more like waterboarding.

Q: Oh Lord.

A: Ha! Don't go looking *there* for docile parenting support. The Judeo-Christian God ran a tight ship! Onto which he let only eight people while drowning the rest of humanity in a flood. Comparatively, He's probably fine with the "pitcher of cold water over the head" method.

A teacher employs a new form of discipline to soothe a riled student. Because if the government won't let you discipline prison— **students** *by standard methods, you need to get creative.*

Q: Is it true that teachers were allowed to beat students?

A: And how! It was well into the twentieth century before teachers stopped disciplining children by whacking them with "The

This "pony boy" is an example of the sort of bench that reform school boys would lie across to receive their birching.

Board of Education." But again, society did not consider this "beating." And of course, most educators took care not to overdo it. After all, as the anonymous author of the 1879 edition of *Manual for Teachers: On Discipline* warns, if you rely too much on corporal punishment, it will lose its effect.

"The commoner it is, the less effective it is," this education expert explains. "It should be administered by the head-teacher in private, or with only a few witnesses. Public corporal punishment has a tendency to brutalize all who take part in it and witness it."

By "brutalize" the author does not mean "hurt all who participate" but rather "reduce participants to a less civilized manner of behavior." Public justice, he explains, will make the boy receiving the punishment more likely to "assume a tone of bravado," forcing the teacher to "engage in an unseemly contest with him."

People in authority know that punishments given in secret are much scarier. And, let's be honest, it's just tidier not to have witnesses.

One Edwin J. Toye, M.D., wrote the *Lancet* editors in October 1901, giving a succinct list of how punishments should be doled out according to offense. It was quite an enlightened view over the previous century's. First, he declares that the habit of beating a scholar's hands with a cane (usually a thin stick of bamboo or other light wood) should be abolished, since it poses a true threat to the bones of the hands and makes the scholar unable to do the work demanded of him. Caning is fine, of course, but only on the back, buttocks, or thighs, and only when inflicted for a sufficient moral reason, not as a penalty for inferior schoolwork.

On the other hand, "Birching [spanking exposed buttocks with a bundle of twigs] is reserved for punishment where some idea of special disgrace is to be attended."

Not all school punishment was the whacking sort, at least not as the Victorian age ebbed into the enlightenment and compassion of the Edwardian age. Simple humiliation was also considered a very useful tool.

Toye is a fan of the Bart Simpson–style punishment of copying out a sentence over and over, as long as what the punishee is writing is relevant to the case, whether it be an apology, reflection of his sins, or simply a proper redo of his homework. Of course, "All written punishments have to pass inspection by the headmaster or his delegate and bear stamp as passed for decent writing and general neatness." He also recommended special paper with a conspicuous pattern or color be used for these written punishments. Employing shame paper made the humiliation public, but discreet.

Speaking of shame paper, it could all be used to fashion the "dunce cap" you've heard so much about. Did you know there was usually a dunce *stool,* as well? Sometimes a whole regatta of dunce accessories! As William B. Smith remembered in an article entitled "Life in Old Virginia 'Befo' de Wah,'" published in a 1910 edition of *The Railway Conductor,* "The old 'dunce cap' was made of paper in the shape of a cone, upon which the word 'dunce' was written. This cap was placed upon the head of the stupid or negligent scholar. The 'dunce stool' was small and three-legged, sometimes called the 'creepy stool.'"

Many writers of the era recall their school's dunce cap as more festive in appearance, trimmed with ribbons and feathers, meant to really drive home how absolutely, clownishly stupid its occupant was. Other schools kept a variety of shame hats, in various sizes, declaring the small head underneath to belong to a "story-teller" (liar), a layabout, or whatever epithet the teacher chose.

Q: Who ever came up with a "dunce cap"? Actually, what in the world is a "dunce," anyway?

The dunce cap could be quickly modified to highlight whatever flaw was most prominent in a child.

A: A fourteenth-century Catholic scholar. You should have known that; come get your "ignorant of Medieval philosophy" cap, young lady.

The dunce cap came into being because society goes through periods of hating Catholics. One such Catholic lived in the 1300s and was named John Duns Scotus. He had some very intelligent and, at the time, popular theories about God and…stuff. He wrote a lot about a theory called Univocity, which considered that the goodness of God was the same goodness found in all things, but it was on a continuum that…ehh…Honestly, I don't entirely understand it. It's pretty deep and would take a bit of study to fully comprehend. And I'll understand if you want to take a moment to appreciate the irony of not being smart enough to understand a Dun(ce).

Duns Scotus's writings were widely read and taught in universities for a while. But eventually Catholics became unpopular again, as did their philosophers. This was the Renaissance, and the philosophy du jour was a new kind of humanism modeled on classical Greek and Roman philosophy, which followers of Duns Scotus (known as Scotists, Dunses, or Dunsmen) categorically rejected.

And so, as an 1855 article entitled "The Geology of Words" explains, "The Duns disciples were villainized as violent opponents of learning, so that a Duns-ist, or Dunse, became the name of contempt for an 'ignorant booby.'"

John Duns Scotus doesn't so much mind the appropriation of his name to mean "stupid" but would prefer you refrain from using the word "booby."

And since the Renaissance marked a shift toward educating young men, and since Catholics and Protestants were much snippier than they are now, a professor berating a young man refusing to get with the program with "Oh, I believe we have a follower of Duns in our midst!" would have been reasonable. The accompanying hat was possibly reminiscent of Duns's monk's cap.

Q: This is really queasy stuff. I understand it was a different world, but I don't know if I have the stomach for Victorian discipline.

A: Then I tell you, with deadly seriousness, you're going to want to skip the next few pages. But I implore you not to. What I have to tell you isn't nice. But it's the truth, and people who want to understand their world don't ignore truth.

The punishments I've described above were among the gentler of their time. They are incomplete, not representing a full picture of child discipline in the Victorian age.

Children were beaten to bruises and welts by even good parents in this era, and that is a fact. Children were killed by bad parents.

We don't know this because of recorded incidents of "child abuse." Legally, in the parts of the world we're focusing on, such a term did not exist until the end of the century. The best way to understand Victorian child discipline is to look at death inquests.

In *Roscoe's Digest of the Law of Evidence in Criminal Cases,* volume 2, published in 1888, Henry Roscoe describes many precedent-setting cases of child death from both England and America. The cases he cites show that children were "accidentally" beaten to death with anguishing frequency. Grown-ups literally got away with murder, thanks to the basic law, applicable the world over, stating, "Parents, masters, and other persons having authority may administer reasonable correction to those under their care, and if death ensue without their fault, it will be no more than accidental death."

Q: Parents beat kids to death and it wasn't even considered their fault?

A: It wasn't a question of fault, but intent. You *were* allowed to use whatever means necessary to get your child in line; you owned your child as surely as you owned your dog. But you weren't allowed to intentionally *kill* your child. So when punishment went too far and a kid ended up dead, a judge had to decide if you'd done it on purpose or not, taking into consideration the age and physical constitution of the child, the degree of provocation the caretaker was subjected to, and, most important, what object was used to beat the child.

Roscoe describes a particular case to illustrate the extenuating circumstances that separate "child-murder" from "tragic accident." "A father whose son had been frequently guilty of thefts, of which complaints had been made, had often corrected him," he writes. "At length the son, being charged with another theft, and...the father in a passion beat his son, by way of chastisement, with a rope."

The boy died from this beating. The bereft father was consumed with sorrow and guilt. He had honestly intended "only to have punished him with such severity as to have cured him of his wickedness. The learned judge who tried the prisoner, after consulting his colleague and the principal counsel on the circuit, ruled this to be manslaughter only."

The court saw a father who was at his wits' end with a wicked son and used an object that one wouldn't normally think of as deadly (as opposed to other cases where boys were disciplined with iron rods or heavy canes, which were viable lethal weapons).

And the punishment for accidentally beating your child, student, or apprentice to death? It varied, "at the discretion of the court." It could be life in prison...or a fine.

Q: That's...I have no words. This is so sick. How could this be allowed?

A: There are a hundred different answers to that question, none of which satisfy. I can tell you that the idea of a child who was "self-governing," obeying from a sense of guilt rather than shame (guilt is what we feel when we know we've been bad; shame is what we feel when we're *caught* being bad), was relatively new. I can explain that these kids lived in a world where everyone who was strong beat up on the weak. Dad beat Mom, the landlord punched Dad, the cops knocked the landlord down in the street...it was an age of the fist. And I can remind you that your own great-great-grandchildren will be asking how *you* could have been so unloved that you were allowed to ride a bicycle on the same street where cars drove, or given the common poison called "refined sugar" as a treat.

None of that really makes it better, I know.

I can give you some satisfaction, though. It was here, during the Victorian era, that children began to become precious and protected.

It all started because of one little girl.

Q: How did one girl change the way children were treated?

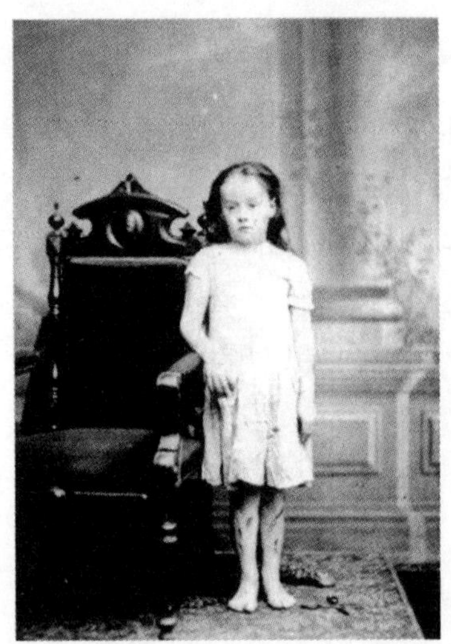
Mary Ellen "Connolly," age ten.

A: Bluntly, child abuse laws, at least in America (England followed suit within decades with its own laws), finally began to change in earnest because of what you might call the perfect case of child abuse, and the public's infatuation with reading about it.

Her name was Mary Ellen Connolly, and she was ten years old. Her story was fairy-tale caliber, complete with wicked stepmother, fairy godmother, and savior in the form of a kind and powerful man.

Once upon a time, on a dark and stormy night in 1874, Mrs. Etta Angell Wheeler (she even had *angel* in her name), a Methodist missionary, was attending a dying woman in a tenement house in New York. It was there, according to Ernest Nusse of an 1885 edition of the *Bay State Monthly*, the dying woman spoke the words that would change the world: "My hours are numbered, but how can I die in peace when night and day I hear the beating by her mother-in-law [foster mother] of the unhappy little girl who lives in the room next to mine?"

Mrs. Wheeler did indeed find an overworked, starved, and beaten orphan named Mary Ellen next door. But she could not find any judicial authority willing to remove her from the Connollys: the man and woman who, though they had no legal proof of it, claimed her as theirs.

Mrs. Wheeler's attempts to save the child were thwarted at every turn by the law, according to Jacob August Riis, who wrote *The Children of the Poor* in 1892. Police, wrote Riis, told her that there wasn't enough evidence that the child's life was in danger to remove her from her "parents." So, Mrs. Wheeler went to private children's charities and well-known philanthropists.

They replied, Riis tells us, "It is a dangerous thing to interfere between parent and child, and you might get yourself into trouble if you did so, as parents are proverbially the best guardians of their own children."

Ah, but beware the tenacious church lady. Mrs. Wheeler was on a mission. She knocked on one last door. "Finally, in despair, she said: 'I will make one more effort to save this child. There is one man in this city who has never turned a deaf ear to the cry of the helpless, and who has spent his life in just this work for the benefit of unoffending animals. I will go to Henry Bergh.'"

Henry Bergh.

Henry Bergh, known as the "Friend of Beasts," was the man who founded the Society for the Prevention of Cruelty to Animals. He reasoned that little Mary Ellen was for all legal intents an animal, owned by the Connollys, with no voice or rights of her own. So, she deserved as much kindness as any animal. He brought Mary Ellen to court to testify against her abusers, wrapped in a horse blanket to drive home the point. There, Mary Ellen gave clear and heartbreaking testimony:

> *My father and mother are both dead. I don't know how old I am...Mamma [Mrs. Connolly] has been in the habit of whipping and beating me almost every day. She used to whip me with a twisted whip—a rawhide. The whip always left a black and blue mark on my body. She struck me with the scissors and cut me; I have no recollection of ever having been kissed by anyone—have never been kissed by Mamma. I have never been taken*

> *on my Mamma's lap and caressed or petted. I never dared to speak to anybody, because if I did I would get whipped...I do not know for what I was whipped—Mamma never said anything to me when she whipped me. I do not want to go back to live with Mamma, because she beats me so.*

The court removed Mary Ellen from the Connollys, and, though there were a few bumps along the way, she grew up to be a contented wife and mother, living a full life and dying in 1956. And in the process, she started a revolution in children's rights.

Q: I'm glad Mary Ellen's story helped other kids, but how is that story "perfect"? To refer to any tale of child abuse as a fairy tale is downright ghoulish.

A: You're right. But humans *are* ghoulish, hungry for lurid details, and fantastic stories that are, as Nusse described Mary Ellen's life of torture and rescue, "both *thrilling and dramatic*."

Consider, Mary Ellen Connolly was one of maybe thousands of children in New York City in 1874 subjected to severe abuse of some sort. Millions of mistreated children came before her. And stories about their suffering didn't sell newspapers or change the world. Why was her story different?

The Victorians were short on pity. Not because they were cruel, but because when you live in a hard world you are able to traverse it better with a hardened heart. They didn't *like* poor people, those dirty and desperate beggars who overran their cities. To many they were a reminder of the life that awaited *them* should their husband fall ill or their job be lost. There was a strongly held belief that if you found yourself in a low station, it was your own fault—perhaps your laziness or just God meting out justice for your secret sins. Homeless children, cheerfully referred to as "street-arabs" and "gutter-snipes," were not spared this judgment.

And while Mary Ellen's captors, the Connollys, fit the prejudiced stereotype of the poor as nasty and vile, *Mary Ellen* was different. She was more like the little heroines of *Grimms' Fairy Tales* and Hans Christian Andersen works, books now translated into English and enjoying wide circulation. More like the children in the novels of Dickens and Alcott, some of the first to be narrated from a virtuous child's point of view. The notion of children as humans, not burdens, was seeping into the collective consciousness just when Mary Ellen made headlines.

Her father had been honorable, a soldier who died in the Union Army. Her mother, though accounts vary, most likely worked herself to death trying to provide for her baby. It was supposed that this woman had either been deceived into giving her daughter over to what she believed was superior care, a baby farm, or the child had been stolen from her on her deathbed.

Q: What in the world is a "baby farm"? Do I even want to know?

A: No. But I will tell you, because, again, it is the truth. Baby farms were like foster homes or orphanages, except completely unregulated and widely considered to be fatal for their inhabitants.

In 1915, one Dr. Woodward described the much-maligned institution as follows:

> *The baby is left with [a woman] and the mother pays two or three dollars a week or a month, as the case may be for a while. The mother may then disappear, leaving the baby in the baby farm. Many of the babies*

In one famous case of baby-farming, the undernourished children were kept in an opium stupor. The proprietress of this particular baby farm, Margaret Waters, was executed in 1870, believed to be responsible for the deaths of nineteen children.

placed in such establishments are placed there possibly with the hope that they will never come out alive. They are illegitimate children, some of them, and others are simply the children of poor women who have burdens that they cannot bear while they are going out to earn their living in kitchens and places of that sort.

"It is unjust to say that all the keepers of baby-farms are as heartless as they are pictured," wrote Dr. George F. Shrady in an 1884 edition of the *Medical Record.* "Many, undoubtedly, are even more pitiless."

Shrady reminds his readers that a high mortality rate is to be expected based on the youth and poverty of the "inmates." That is not what makes the institution so criminal. It's when you add "improper food, poor sanitary arrangements, lack of care and proper inspection" that the death rate "becomes a frightful one. The whole aim of the typical baby-farmer is to make as much as possible with the least expenditure of time, labor, and money."

Older children, who would have been of particularly hardy stock to have made it to toddler age, might be adopted out of such places. Some historians believe that was Mary Ellen's roundabout route to belonging to the Connollys. Thankfully, one of the many positive repercussions of Mary Ellen's case was to raise awareness about baby farms, leading to a crackdown.

Q: So the public was primed for a "princess in rags" fairy tale, and Mary Ellen had good timing. What else made her sad story "perfect"?

A: Mary Ellen further galvanized the protective spirit of the public by the lack of (reported) sexual abuse, which would have made her story unpublishable and sullied her in the minds of the public.

Q: Wait. Come on. Society would rally for a girl beaten to a pulp but not a molested one?

A: Like I said, this is rough stuff. Victorians had very deep and conflicted attitudes toward sexuality. Maybe because they lived in such a rough world, they were obliged to put so much value in purity and innocence.

No one would consciously blame a child for sexual abuse, but it would make it a very different story. Would the adults feel it so important to save this Forlorn Innocent if she'd already lost that innocence? Her story would go from scandalous to debauched. From scintillating to disgusting. It wasn't fair. It just *was*.

Instead, Mary Ellen had bruises and cuts made from scissors, right there in plain view below her tattered nightdress. A pretty, white, nonimmigrant child who spoke clearly and humbly of her trials.

Add the aforementioned ingredients of her noble champions, Wheeler, Bergh, and the dying old lady, and you had the world's attention and outrage. Had social media existed, thousands would have stepped forward with their own #maryellen stories, inspired by the child's bravery.

Q: And kids were safer? I could really use a happy ending here.

A: I think they were safer. Perhaps most significantly, the case led to Bergh's creation of the New York Society for the Prevention of Cruelty to Children.

By the time of Nusse's article, nine years after Mary Ellen's case, the NYSPCC had "investigated 13,077 complaints, involving 53,308 children, prosecuted 4,035 cases, convicted 3,637

offenders, rescued and placed in homes or institutions 7,555 children." That was just in New York. Other states immediately followed suit, as did other countries, creating advocacy and safety for children. It was imperfect, it remains so, but it was an incalculable improvement.

More than that, Mary Ellen triggered an avalanche of concern for child welfare that had never before existed. Child labor laws began to appear throughout America and Europe, though it would take a few decades for them to become universal in Western society.

This 1880 illustration shows the growing public intolerance of cruelty to children after Mary Ellen. Among laws passed in New York to protect kids were those forbidding them from being used in circus, theater, and gymnastic acts.

In truth there was still a long way to go. But Mary Ellen cut the path for millions of children to follow.

Q: I'm glad. I guess. Just…this is the worst chapter. In the world. The absolute worst.

A: You're a mollycoddle, and you should be forever thankful for it. Remember, these children were born into a world of war and hunger and danger. They needed to be made of stern stuff.

Let us take a hypothetical: Say young Master Alfred is setting out at age sixteen to apprentice as a skilled laborer in a factory. Not a bad placement at all, sure to bring him a respectable middle-class life.

Imagine him raised as he would be today. Taught to try his best, but that mistakes happen and that's okay. Taught that he's special and deserving of gentle treatment and respect as his basic human right. Taught to take "second chances" and fail-safes for granted.

When he makes an error in measurement (because the birch and the dunce cap hadn't fostered a bone-deep anxiety that causes him to thrice-check his work), a whole shipment's worth of wood is cut wrong and rendered useless. If he's not fired immediately with no recommendation (and no prospects without one), his fellow employees will hate him, as all their wages have been docked due to lost revenue. Since he has no familiarity with physical pain, or the importance of keeping your dignity while enduring it, when they grab him after work to take their anger out on him, he'll be unprepared to either fight back or spring back emotionally once he's defeated.

Will he go to Human Resources and file a complaint of harassment? File a personal assault charge that will do nothing more than amuse the police, who spend every day knee-deep in putrid human misery? Will he demand audience with his employer and explain that he tried his best? No. Not here, not now.

We can afford mistakes in the twenty-first century, because our world is well padded. We can indulge a level of sensitivity that used to be allowed only the smallest of children.

However harsh it seems to us today, many of the Victorians' disciplinary methods *did* help prepare children for the pitiless place that was to be their home.

Q: This chapter makes me feel like someone birched my heart. I'm...not going to use anything I learned here in disciplining my twenty-first-century child. Unless you can tell me something nice?

Guidance as discipline. "And so you see, Tabitha, putting morphine in Mrs. Walling's tea is only fun until we have to figure out how to get her off the floor before Father comes home."

A: Of course! Remember, times were changing!

An article from an 1886 edition of *Good Housekeeping* shows the sway of the new thought, reminding readers that "over-discipline is as harmful as the lack of discipline."

"Many a time by forbidding we create a desire," writes the author, Rose Dalton, "often the thing forbidden is of little consequence compared with the train of evils its prohibition introduces. When the child has disobeyed it is punished; the next time it disobeys it naturally tells a falsehood to avoid punishment."

Most of the bad things a very small child does are done innocently out of excitement or because they have the IQ of a two-year-old. (And are simply teeming with Original Sin, of course.) That sort of misbehaving should be gently corrected, the child neither beaten with footwear nor mildly waterboarded.

Instead, says Dalton, "To make our discipline effectual we must walk beside them, and guide and help them, sympathizing with them in their failures, not-constantly holding their faults before them."

The goal in the late nineteenth century was to have a self-governing child. One who, as Dalton puts it, "obeys from a sense of honor, rather than from fear of the consequences."

Q: Wait...Rose Dalton was a real person? From *Titanic*? I'm not listening to anything that woman says. There was SO room for both her and Jack on that door.

A: *Dalton.* Not *Dawson.* Kate Winslet's character was not real and it wasn't a question of space on the dang door; it was a question of water displacement and the buoyancy of solid oak that...Just... never mind. That's not an issue here.

Q: Yeah, but Jack would have been such a great dad...

A: Okay, Dear One. Shhh now. It's all right. This was a difficult chapter, wasn't it? It's causing your mind to seek protection in more pleasant places. Like one of the...greatest naval tragedies in history.

Now let's put aside this unpleasantness and talk about something fun. Like math and menstruation. Can you do both at the same time? Let's see!

6

How Do I Raise a Menstruating Daughter Without Causing Brain Damage, Nerve Failure, or General Impudence?

And Other Thoughts on Education

Q: Okay. When they weren't being birched or caned, what kind of education did Victorian children receive?

A: Oh, heavens. We're going to have to break that down into smaller questions, based on which part of the century, what part of the world, social class, and what qualifies as education. For instance, "Did Victorian girls receive formal education?" is a nice tight question to start off with.

Q: Why am I not surprised to learn that girls received a different education from boys?

A: Because you've been paying attention and have surmised that nothing in the nineteenth century was gender neutral or gender inclusive (except certain pretty, pretty dresses which we'll learn about later). But in this case, it's not just about whether or not girls would get the same education as boys (which of course they wouldn't—don't be obtuse). Education *itself* was new!

In fact, the belief that all children must be "educated" is, historically, still so fresh that we're not sure it won't eventually be ruled a fad.

For most of history, "education" as we know it just didn't matter. World history, literature, sensitivity training—it was all useless to the average human, of either gender. You did not collect knowledge just for the sake of clogging your mind with it. You learned the skills that would help you survive.

Before the nineteenth century, people on both sides of the Atlantic had little time for or interest in what could be learned in books.

Reading simply wasn't necessary to a good life. Just look at documents left by successful, wealthy men—you'll see an "X" and the words "his mark" scrawled in place of a signature. You could thrive in America and never even know how to write your own name.

Replica of 1851 "His Mark" signature of Nicolaus Allan, a successful though illiterate businessman who catered to California gold rushers.

Q: How could something as simple as reading be unimportant to successful living?

A: Simple, my Aunt Fanny! It took you years to learn to do it good.

Q: "Do it *well*."

A: Don't be cheeky. Success was possible, at least partly, because of small, immobile populations.

Contracts and businesses could be conducted on handshakes. If your grandfather had done business with the Miller family (and, yes, they were called the Millers because they had owned the town mill for generations) as his grandfather before him did, you knew the character of the man you worked with. And he knew if he cheated you, the whole town would find out and stop doing business with him.

Furthermore, Jack Miller Jr. did not need to know how to read to run the mill he'd one day inherit. *But he did need an exhaustive education.* He needed to learn to judge the potential knot and grain imperfection of a board just by looking at the tree it came from. How to keep a saw blade sharp, and what precautions to take to keep his machinery running should the river that powers it shrink from drought. Not to mention math for budgeting and multiple units of measurement. He had to know all of that, *plus* what every man was expected to know just to survive: how to care for his animals, how to repair (or even build) his home, how to judge weather conditions by looking at the horizon or monitoring the crick in his old mother's knee.

He was *highly* educated by the time he came into manhood. It was just a very *specific* education.

Q: What about women?

A: His wife was highly educated too. She knew willow-bark tea brought fever down and where to find the maggots needed to help clear festering wounds. She knew how to feed twelve people with five ears of corn and two dead rabbits, which she could also catch, kill, and dress with a few flicks of her wrist. She could lay out the geometrical pattern pieces to create her husband's pantaloons, join the fabric with nothing but a sharp sliver of metal and thread she spun herself from her own sheep. *This* was education, intensive and applicable beyond what most of us will ever encounter.

But books? Books, perhaps save the family Bible, were for dandies. For useless men who did not use their hands to earn their bread, and women who were so idle that they needed whimsical distraction from long-dead storytellers and poets. Only the wealthiest homes had libraries, filled with hand-bound books, each one a painstakingly printed work of art. A home library was a curiosity, a place an accomplished man would receive visitors and supplicants. This wasn't a room from which you actually selected books to read—after all, the books of any moral or intellectual value were written in European languages, or ancient Greek or Latin. The home library (the only kind there was for most of history) was the equivalent of a fully equipped in-home Pilates studio: a sign of

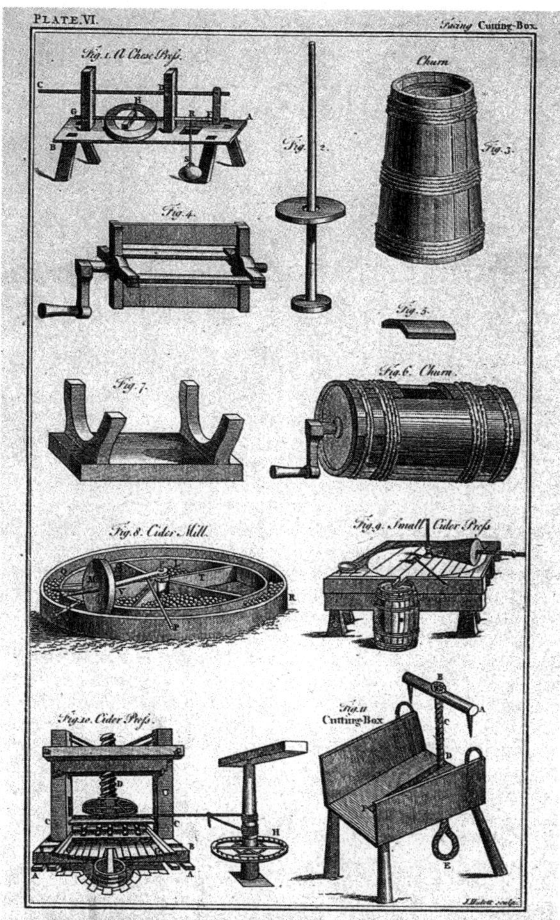

Quick: identify, construct, and then use all these tools to keep yourself from starving. No idea? And you think you're educated!

wealth and class, great for showing off...but mostly just a place you could go to be alone and get drunk.

Q: I just can't imagine a world without books.

A: I'm glad you feel that way. But early books weren't terribly fun. Novels written in modern English didn't even show up until the 1600s, and they weren't abundant. *Don Quixote* and *Robinson Crusoe* were popular, if you were the sort to sully your mind with fictitious frippery. More acceptable were books with religious themes and historical lessons, like Bunyan's *Pilgrim's Progress* or the works of Milton. Well, maybe not Milton. Unless you're willing to overlook his blasphemy that Satan's existence was part of God's design. And you can forget about Chaucer, popular even though it was written in Middle English. "The Miller's Tale"? Pure pornography laced with scatological humor. By today's standards the man of the house would have kept it in a buried file on his computer marked "Power Tool Warranties."

Q: So why did reading suddenly become important?

A: It came creeping through the homes of the wealthy over the centuries, but it was the Victorian era, also the industrial era, when literacy pounced on the masses. Printing presses were cheaper to own and easier to operate. Ease of distribution (books were heavy and weren't worth their weight in cargo holds) came with the trains and new roads that sprouted up all over the world. Books began to matter as industrial changes created more free time to write and read them. Engineers and scientists could learn what would have taken years of research and study under a master of the art (see, that term used to mean something) in a single tome.

Also, you could now do business with men *outside* your own town. Writing letters was not new, but affordable paper and ink were, and new post offices were sprouting up around the American Colonies. In 1790, there were only seventy-five post offices in the whole country, and they were not well regulated. (To be fair, at that point "America" ended at the Mississippi River, and though technically we were in possession of Wisconsin and part of what

An illustration from Chaucer's Canterbury Tales, *wherein a man woos a woman in a fashion described as having "caughte hire by the queynte." Poorly. Woos her* poorly.

would be Minnesota, those weren't popular destinations for mail. Or people.)

Western Europe of course had a more advanced mail system to match its millennia of established towns and travel routes. But it still was the norm, clear until the Industrial Revolution, to remain in your own town or part of your city, plying your great-grandfather's trade, perfectly illiterate, throughout your life.

But how quickly the nineteenth century changed all that. For instance, by 1860, America had 28,498 post offices. The American postal system became one of the most important government offices, as the only way to ensure long-distance communication in a wild and growing country. By 1831, postal employees accounted for 76 percent of the civilian federal workforce. Postmasters outnumbered soldiers 8,764 to 6,332 and were the most widespread representatives of the federal government.

And all *this* is why you suddenly, for the first time in history, needed to know how to read and write. Why you needed "school" for your children.

There were too many people, too many machines creating idleness and books, and a damnable influx of post offices. By the second quarter of the nineteenth century, if your son ever intended to use the mail, do more than menial labor, or avoid becoming some milch-cow for a no-good fobbing whisper-dubber (fall victim to fraud due to his ignorance) he had better learn to read.

Q: And daughters too, of course. People didn't want their daughters to be milch-cow fob dubs either, right?

A. That's not how you say it. But, true, by the nineteenth century, if you were of any position but the lowest and poorest, you would indeed want your daughter to be able to read, write, and do basic arithmetic. After all, she would one day be the mistress of a household, which would require her to be able to budget, write notes to grocers, read the Bible to children, and proffer invitations to other wives that might further her husband's career. The question was how to best mold her fragile mind.

Q: The same way a boy's mind was molded?

A: I don't know what about this book has led you to believe that I'm going to answer that in the affirmative. In fact, we both know I'm probably going to say something wildly sexist. For instance, it's impolitic to notice, but...how can one *avoid* seeing the connection between the breakneck decline of our society and women going to college?

Q: That's actually even more sexist than I expected. Congratulations.

A: The female mind, it's a tender thing. Your daughter has got enough to worry about as a developing young woman as it is. Her

"Oh, Sadie! I only tear up your books to help you stay rooted in the reality of your family and home! Now don't pout—have some laudanum."

body is blossoming, awkwardly and painfully, into one of the only natural vessels that can create and sustain new life. Isn't that a big enough job all by itself?

Please don't mistake me: almost all experts of the Victorian era believed a young girl should have some education. But how much, and what kind? And how might we apply the finest bits of what the Victorians knew about female education to our own daughters today? There is evidence...of a sort...that overeducating girls caused them great harm, if you're willing to look at it.

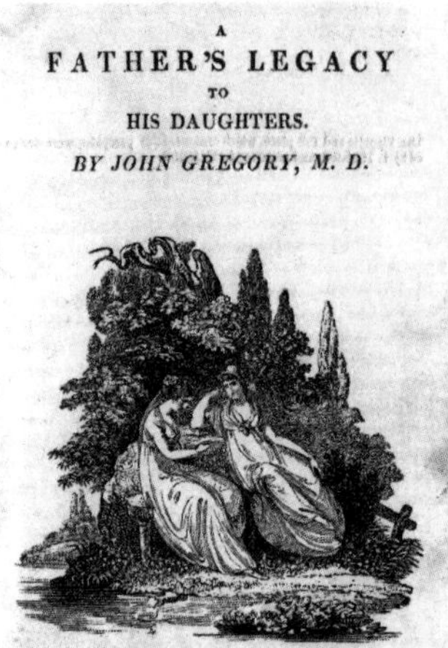
A
FATHER'S LEGACY
TO
HIS DAUGHTERS.
BY JOHN GREGORY, M. D.

STOURPORT,
PRINTED AND SOLD, BY G. NICHOLSON.
1815.

"D'ya ever get the feeling that Dad's...kind of a dillweed?"

Q: Like I'm willing to look at a train wreck. I don't want to...but I can't help it.

A: Super! Some of the more devoted parents of the era, men who knew the way of the world and how inadequately women fit into it, would counsel their daughters to embrace a façade of ignorance if not the actual condition itself. Take John Gregory, who wrote *A Father's Legacy to His Daughters* in 1774. His book and the advice within aged well and was reprinted liberally as a guide for young women far into the nineteenth century.

Gregory knew that most people preferred women as they existed in paintings. Remember, ladies in paintings don't talk. They don't even look like they're about to talk, or ever *have* talked. That's not a coincidence, said Gregory. Because when real women do, they irritate everyone in the room.

He warned against engaging in sharp or clever wordplay with men. "Wit is the most dangerous talent you can possess: it must be guarded with great discretion and good-nature, otherwise it will create you many an enemy."

Having a sense of humor is another way to disgrace yourself.

"Humor...is often a great enemy to delicacy, and a still greater one to dignity of character. It may sometimes gain you applause, but will never procure you respect."

And whatever you do, never let a man suspect you're as smart as he is. Well, you aren't as smart as he is, obviously: your brainpan is too small and likely engorged with fantasies of new frocks and fuzzy ducklings. But don't let him suspect you're smart even for a woman. "If you happen to have any learning, keep it a profound secret," says Gregory, "especially from the men, who generally look with a jealous and malignant eye on a woman of great parts and a cultivated understanding." In conclusion, strive to emulate an especially quiet yet engaging toddler. Otherwise, warns Gregory, "It will be thought you assume superiority over the rest of the company."

"'Rectum?' says the doctor. 'Forget that, it damn near KILLED 'im!'" Maren's skilled verbal wordplay often went unappreciated in mixed company.

Q: That's intolerable, ridiculous advice.

A: Now it is, maybe. Gregory no doubt honestly intended this advice for his daughters' own good. The things his daughters would need to do, need to be, in order to have a contented life were very different from what we imagine for our children today. The question is, should his advice be dismissed out of hand, or are we brave enough to take a closer look at the potential process and dangers of female education?

Q: Oh, by all means! So how much education can my daughter take before the pressure of knowledge shrivels her womb?

A: Ah, now we're on the same page! How you educated your daughter in the 1800s depended, not surprisingly, on your wealth and social station. People of the middle or merchant class often relied on "dame schools," a system so agreeable that it is still in use today, though it's intended for younger children and we call

Both genders received healthy doses of shame along with basic education while attending local "dame schools."

it preschool or daycare. A (preferably literate) woman of reputable character would take five to ten small children into her home during the day and provide them with some instruction while she went about her housework. Dame schools were an inexpensive and reasonable option at a time when public schools were not available (schooling would not become compulsory in Britain until the late 1800s and would not become law in all the American states until the twentieth century), and parents were not able to teach. Here the children learned to read, write, and do basic arithmetic.

Q: Girls are allowed to learn *math?* Well, goose my bustle!

A: No. *Arithmetic,* not math. Adding and subtracting, multiplying and dividing, the equations you'll actually *use* in your lifetime. *Mathematics* was and is an entirely different study, involving intangible geometric proofs, algebraic formulae, and the slow death of a young person's self-confidence. Only the most advanced (male) scholars officially studied mathematics at this time. That custom has changed. For some exorable reason. Well, perhaps I'm too prejudicial against mathematics. You have no doubt used the advanced trigonometry you studied in high school many times while employing parallax methods to calculate the distance between planets. Or maybe that time you were adjusting radiological emissions to eliminate cancer cells? Oh, those aren't among your hobbies? Yet you gave up two years of your precious youth and shed unnumbered tears of rage to learn them? Then forgot them immediately because they had no practical application in your life? And so it will be for your own children, if you abide by modern educational mores.

All it takes for evil to conquer is for generations of good people to not stand up and say, "I never once used any math beyond long division."

But back to a simpler time. A girl would leave a dame school whenever it was no longer worth her parents' money or time to keep her there, usually around age ten. There were no set lessons or graduation requirements, which, as we will see later, was a pivotal problem in female education.

Q: Did they go to high school, or some equivalent at least?

A: Not in the earlier part of the century. In the 1700s and before, if a man of means took a notion to have his daughter educated, she would first have a governess, usually a learned young woman whose family had fallen on hard times, requiring her to work. Or, for more esoteric knowledge, she might have sat private lessons with a male tutor, as the famous Eloise did with her teacher and lover, Abelard. Possibly this wasn't the best system, at least in their case. It ended with Eloise acquiring both a strong grasp of the classics and a bastard child, after which she lived her life out in a convent. And Abelard...well, he had testicles *before* Eloise's family found out what she was really learning in those tutoring sessions... not so much after.

But that was rare. After a governess had taught all she had to offer, there was the question of what was next for your daughter. Marriage before the age of eighteen was considered gauche even in the nineteenth century. So the question was, where might we stick a teenage girl to preserve her virtue, improve her marriageability, and not have to put up with her moping and pouting? If only there were some sort of...live-in daycare for moody teenagers.

Abelard to Eloise: "Honey, no dad ever really *means it when he threatens to chop off your boyfriend's jewels and send you to a nunnery! Relax!"*

Q: Was there some sort of live-in daycare for moody teenagers?

A: Indeed there was! At least for rich girls. Most girls were not rich—those girls could consider their education complete by the age of twelve or fourteen. By that time, no matter what educational route she took—learning from her parents, dame school, governess, or one of the few publicly funded coed schools starting to crop up over the Western world—she would be able to read and do household sums, and have a thorough religious indoctrination, enough learning for girls of any class to get by well enough in the nineteenth century. So, in their early teens, girls would find work on farms and factories, be placed as servants, take jobs as village teachers or governesses, or stay home and learn housekeeping from their mothers.

But for many parents, status-conscious ones especially, that wasn't enough.

These parents didn't want their teen daughters to go to *universities* or anything like that. But they might have a better shot at landing "the right sort" of gentleman if they mastered skills that only women of the leisure classes could turn their attention to: music, dancing, decorative needlepoint ("fancywork," as opposed to utilitarian "plain work"), and, of course, religious indoctrination.

Q: How did you know if you were sending your girl to a quality boarding school?

A: That question vexed parents, even then. These ladies' seminaries/academies/finishing schools were, at least for the first part of the nineteenth century, nothing more than dame schools for big girls. Once again, a lady, usually a spinster, hopefully of sterling reputation and refinement, would hang out her shingle, and take thirty or so girls between the ages of twelve and eighteen into her home. There she would keep them, and teach them…whatever.

AUGUSTA FEMALE SEMINARY.

STAUNTON, VA.

Miss Mary Julia Baldwin, Principal.

THE ACADEMIC TERM OF THIS INSTITUTION begins the middle of SEPTEMBER each year, and closes the middle of the following JUNE.

This is the largest first class Institution in Virginia: It has a corps of upwards of twenty officers and teachers. The English course more extensive and thorough than elsewhere found in female schools. Advantages for music and languages cannot be surpassed. Seven music teachers—four instrumental and three vocal—are constantly employed, whose reputation has extended wherever the school is known.

A resident French governess and French gentleman teach the pupils to speak the language, as well as read and write it.

The buildings for comfort, elegance and convenience, unsurpassed by any in the South.

A new building, eighty-six by fifty feet, containing recitative rooms, music rooms, dining hall, with a chapel admirably adapted to music, will be completed by the 13th September.

The character and reputation of the School may be learned from the annexed testimonials from gentlemen whose position and character give value to their commendations:

"I can honestly advise parents to send their children to this excellent Institution, which I regard as a great public blessing.

"JOSEPH R. WILSON,
"Columbia, S. C."

The Augusta Female Seminary advertises unsurpassed instruction in music and French. It is assumed some arithmetic and dishwashing courses are available to the less comely students.

"Another letter from my Prudie just arrived! I'd invite you to read it but it's in French so—"
"Cram it, Helen."

There was no standardized curriculum for girls. In an attempt to attract more pupils and more money, many schools tended to focus fervently on the skills that a girl's parents could show off to their neighbors.

Q: Why didn't they take the opportunity to actually *teach* those girls instead of babysitting them?

A: And what should they be taught in a world where your main education centered on the career you would have? In a world where your career was *to be a woman.*

It was in the interest of these schools to teach skills that could be shown off. They wanted mothers of their students to pressure others into attendance through good old-fashioned bragging. "Have you seen the woven picot needle-lace handkerchief my little Prudie made for me? Miss Pueper's Academy insists their girls master even the most complex fancywork. You can always tell a true lady by her throw pillows, don't you agree? How is your little Fideline faring with her stitching? She has such thick, sturdy fingers! Has she mastered that tricky 'threading the needle' part yet? Well, don't fret! Really, delicacy can be quite a curse in a daughter. You're so fortunate that your Fideline is such a solid little trout of a girl!" Of course, Fideline would be enrolled for the next term at Pueper's Girls' Academy.

Q: It sounds like a big con.

A: Precisely. Chaotic, too. There was no governing institution for female education, no graduation requirements, no requirements at all, really. Until 1819, when a woman named Emma Willard, who ran a school like the ones mentioned above, began to believe that the pitiful excuse of an education being offered the girls of America could be considered dangerous to society.

Women were half the population. A mother was (ostensibly) a child's first teacher. Perhaps it was unseemly for women to show the extent of their intelligence in public, but they at least had to be smart enough so that, if asked, they'd have more to offer in a conversation than a handful of slack-jawed Ralph Wiggum–isms.

Q: Go, Emma! Smash the patriarchy!

A: I said "1819," my adorable lil' radical third-wave feminist. Emma made no attempt to smash anything, because Emma knew that would not work in her world. Instead, she pointed out how unsound, how unwholesome, the system was, and how it might be improved.

"My cat's breath smells like cat food."

Willard wrote a concise essay, "A Plan for Improving Female Education," to be presented before the New York Legislature. (Not by her personally, of course; women had no business roaming the halls of government.) In it, she detailed what she saw as the barriers to young women's mental development and, by extension, society's development. It was a much-lauded work and one of the first to argue that a woman's mind was a strong and useful contributor to society. *If treated with proper respect and gentility.*

One problem with girls' schools, she said, was that women usually opened them out of financial need rather than passion for education.

They were not endowed by patrons the way boys' schools were. Preceptresses (lady principals) were at the mercy of their charges and their charges' parents and were encouraged to "teach to the test." "The test" in this case was becoming a pious, dainty-footed ballroom dancer who knew what all the forks at a fancy table setting were for and could speak a bit of French. While sketching fruit.

And, since girls' schools had to save money whenever possible to turn any profit, most of them were cramped houses full of noise and chaos, lacking libraries, ventilation, or many of the other conditions considered necessary to healthy living.

It went without saying that sexually mature girls (over twelve years old) were to be taught only by ladies (see "How Abelard Lost His Scrotum," above). But many of these ladies had never had a thorough education themselves. Besides that, since "teachers" in "schools" for girls had no one overseeing them, no one to report to, you really had no idea what your child might be learning and from whom.

Demoiselle would love to educate your daughter in "the French arts."

Says Willard: "Instances have lately occurred, in which women of bad reputation, at a distance from scenes of their former life, have been entrusted by our unsuspecting citizens with the instruction of their daughters."

All too easily parents assumed that women who could speak French and recite John Donne's "Death Be Not Proud" couldn't possibly be of low character! (Unless, as we've established, they were French. In which case you could almost *guarantee* them to be sensuous deviants.)

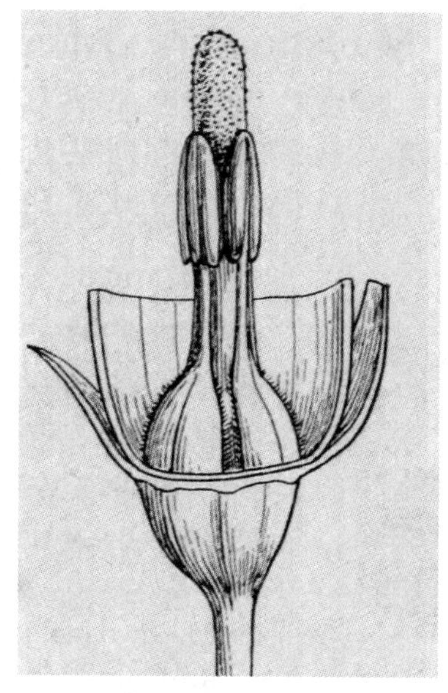

Cross-section of plant reproductive system. Which shows why we must be very careful in teaching our daughters biology: prevalence of plant penises.

Willard wanted better for women. She wanted to create institutions that "might possess the respectability, permanency, and uniformity" of boys' schools, "and yet differ from them, so as to be adapted to that difference of character and duties, to which the softer sex should be formed."

Willard did *not* consider the sexes indistinguishable in their education needs. She wasn't advocating equality. She, and this was realistic of her, didn't see the point of girls becoming masters of ancient languages or trigonometry, or even biology unless it was delicately taught. (We can talk about flowers, they're nice. Just...not the stamen part. Or pistils. None of that filth.)

Willard's lesson plan was practical for her era. Girls would learn subjects falling under four main tenets, pass standardized tests, and graduate. The child would attend a *real* school, overseen by a trustee board, or even by local government, and held accountable to standards outside those of show-offy parents wishing to impress the neighbors. The tenets were, in order of importance:

1. Religious and moral.
2. Literary.
3. Domestic.
4. Ornamental.

"Religious and moral" are self-explanatory. "Literary," in this context, meant *anything* that could be learned out of a book, including science.

Domestic study, the third tenet, would actually prepare a girl for her career. Running a household in the nineteenth century was like running a complicated business. Even if they had servants to do the actual work, girls must learn about that work. Particularly budgeting, the basics of cooking and cleanliness (if these things were not done right, people could get sick and die), how to communicate with tradesmen, how to repair and mend anything in her household, and the basics of infant care to combat an infant mortality rate too depressing to mention. And finally, those Ornamentals. Music, dancing, fancywork, grace in movement, all the things that distinguish a lady from a flap-teated fishwife. It was absolutely revolutionary that Willard thought those of *least* importance.

Educators responded well to Willard's essay. But while society marched forward in the attempt to educate girls, it didn't quite march in the direction Willard intended. Strangely enough, boys and girls began to be educated together as more and more governments decided to pay for them to do so. The reason being, it was simply cheaper to educate both genders together. They might enter through separate doors, sit segregated, and be discouraged from socializing, but they could all learn decimals at the same time.

Or could they?

Q: Yeah. They really can. I've seen it done.

A: As small children, perhaps. And the glum, glazed-eyed gender-rejecting youth of the twenty-first century, maybe. But what about proper girls, who have entered puberty? Even if Victorians could accept that young women's brains were as capable of learning as men's, only a madman would fail to consider

As in this turn-of-the-century Washington, DC, school, it was more cost efficient to educate both genders at once.

the part menstruation plays in a young woman's ability to read books and do math.

Q: You've got to be kidding me.

A: Argue with my cited bibliography! For instance, when John Thorburn wrote *Female Education from a Physiological Point of View* in 1884, long after the gender integration of the school systems and the slow burgeoning of coed universities, he gave voice to what everybody was secretly thinking.

Girls aren't dumb, but their periods turn them into manic-depressive idiots.

And for their own sake, they need to get out of the classroom. "Since my attention was specially called to the subject some years ago," Thorburn wrote, "I have come across a very large number of cases where the growing school girl had been temporarily or permanently injured by scholastic work performed during the menstrual period."

"Everyone just hold it together. We can start crying and smashing stuff again as soon as the photographer leaves."

Thorburn goes on to describe a typical case. An adolescent daughter is brought to him, suffering from any one of the well-known period-related diseases: anemia, hysteria, being excessively moody or sullen and showing deranged appetite (then as now, the unabashed female craving for pickled vegetables or nutmeg was a sure sign of an overtaxed mind and uterus). Today we are tempted to define this behavior in oversimplified terms, terms like "teenager." Medical men of the nineteenth century knew better: these were clearly symptoms of brain degeneration due to overuse.

In most schools, said Thorburn, headmistresses and teachers will sensibly allow girls to forgo heavy study during her period. But of course, they can only grant such leniency to girls who *complain,* as most well-bred girls will not do, especially about this shameful aspect of their lives.

So, the inevitable happens. Said Thorburn, "It was only towards the end of the [school] session that they broke down, but they were often in the end the greatest sufferers from nerve prostration. Two cases of this kind have ended in sudden death from hematocele [bleeding so severe it overflows the uterus and drowns the abdominal cavity], soon after their return home, and several have had local diseases of a troublesome and chronic nature which have taken years to remedy or have never been remedied at all."

Q: Girls bled to death because the strain of education conflicted with the strain of having a uterus?

A: Yes! Maybe! It was written in a book, so probably! Even if a young woman was fortunate enough to survive education without a deadly hemorrhage, the resulting race of females would be wizened, sickly, and prone to madness. If menstruating women continued to be educated, one Dr. Edward Clarke warned, "it requires no prophet to foretell that the wives who are to be mothers in our republic must be drawn from transatlantic homes."

Q: What did doctors who were women say?

A: Mostly they said, "Would you like to see the pillow I embroidered? I'm not a doctor because women aren't allowed in most medical schools and even if they were only jaded hags with no prospects would attend."

With exceptions.

Dr. Mary Putnam Jacobi went about becoming a doctor in a roundabout way, since no direct course was available. She served as a medical aide during the Civil War, studied directly under our nation's first female doctor, Elizabeth Blackwell, and got degrees from a pharmacy school and the Female Medical College of Pennsylvania, neither of which proved sufficient to qualify her to practice medicine. She then fought her way into the École de Médecine

Dr. Jacobi proves once and for all that some women find their periods uncomfortable, some of the time.

of the University of Paris, becoming its second female graduate.

Jacobi knew that her work had to be superior to even be considered in the medical community. Her research was exhaustive, her focus on women's health timely. She won an award from Harvard for a medical dissertation called "The Question of Rest for Women During Menstruation" in 1877. The essay was unusually scientific for the era. Jacobi used sample populations, control groups, measurements, means and medians... Really, she went overboard, considering all a male physician needed to say to give credence to his medical pronouncements was "We have heard..."

She did a study to settle the question of whether or not a woman needed to take it especially easy when she was menstruating, particularly with regard to study and deep thinking. The results Jacobi found were considered definitive, she being an actual woman. But her results weren't terribly conclusive.

The science showed...some women have bad periods and some women don't, and most ladies, save those who suffer violently, just plug along despite their discomfort.

Shrug.

However, as the Devil may cite Scripture for his purposes, so could Mrs. Jacobi's study bend to fit the agenda of whichever writer was quoting her. As in the case of Ely Van de Warker, commissioner of schools for Syracuse, New York, who wrote the extremely pointed essay "Woman's Unfitness for Higher Co-Education" in 1903.

He wrote:

> *Dr. Mary Putnam Jacobi, in her book on* The Question of Rest for Women, *is obliged to reluctantly confess that forty five per cent of women suffer from menstrual pain. Experience [Warker here refers to his own, not Jacobi's study] also shows that twenty per cent of other women suffer from mental depression, lassitude, loss of appetite, and a general sense of physical ill.*

Boom. Mic drop. Women have periods. And almost *half* of them find it uncomfortable. No school for them.

Q: Did this apply to all women, or just scholars? Like, did factory owners give time off to women to overcome their menstruation?

A: Dearheart, we are more than halfway through this book. By now you must have internalized that most rules laid forth in it apply to rich white people rather exclusively. And even then...Irish, Belgians...yecch.

Of course that didn't mean women of the *working class* should cease *their* activities. Ha-ha! Let's not get carried away, now. The female body is designed to withstand menstrual discomfort when the needs of others are in question. We could reinforce this scientifically, but why bother? Women have been scrubbing dishes since people were eating mastodon meat off them. And they haven't died out yet!

It's different when the brain is concerned. A "marked increase in arterial blood-pressure just before, with an abrupt fall after [the menstrual period's] completion" straight up depletes blood and protein and moral stamina intended for the brain.

Q: So...she can menstruate, or she can think stuff. Not both.

A: Precisely! The smarter the woman, the more dangerous it was for her to try to keep up with the boys. As Dr. George J. Engelmann

Happy laundry girls work whether menstruating, pregnant, or riddled with leprosy, and they LOVE it!

put it in *The American Girl of To-day: The Influence of Modern Education on Functional Development,* "The brightest mind, the most sensitive, highstrung, nervous organization is, as a rule, the most responsive and most liable to impairment during the menstrual period."

One day, she's the best in the class...but next week? You'll find her sprawled over her desk sobbing about a dead pigeon she saw on the way to school, silently embarrassing the whole room because they know the only explanation is that she's currently, at that moment, sloughing her womb lining onto a roughly pinned flannel towel. And once you've got that picture in your head, how can you be expected to look that girl in the eye again?

Q: Wow. Do you think I can use that excuse next time I want a shift off work? "Sorry, I'm using all my mind powers to slough my womb lining. It's trickier than you'd think. Can't come in today."

A: Sadly, no. Not anymore. That gentle and sensible world has fallen from us, and women's special needs are often overlooked. Girls are now educated and treated almost exactly as boys are. Of course, the proper rearing of boys has also fallen by the wayside, as we shall see in the next chapter.

7

My Young Son Refuses to Engage in Fisticuffs or Play Games with Greased Livestock. Is It Too Late to Prevent His Inevitable Homosexuality?

On Turning Boys into Men

Today, in many preschools, there exists a discipline tool called the Peace Corner. This is where children are directed when disagreements arise. For example, two boys at odds over whose turn it is to use the class loom to continue weaving ethically sheared alpaca fibers into endearingly lopsided potholders to be donated to the less fortunate would go to the Peace Corner to settle the score. There, they would take turns holding the "talking stick" or the "rose of peace" or the "tape dispenser of empathy" and give voice to their woes. Eventually compromise is reached ("Skyler will use the loom until five songs on the 'Fife and Rainforest Howling for Toddlers' classroom playlist have played, and then it can be Maddox's turn!") and everyone is a winner.

Lucius tells himself that the birds are more afraid of him than he is of them... but they're not.

Have mercy upon your poor little eunuch. However noble your intentions, this is no way to bring up a boy.

What a peculiar era to raise a son in today. We equate the masculine boy with the bully, the swaggering buffoon incapable of empathy or respect for anyone different than himself. So we fill our son's toy box with gender-neutral wooden toys and we make sure that whichever superhero he's chosen to focus his life on has a fleshed-out backstory to explain his violent tendencies. (Deadpool has been through *a lot*, guys.)

We raise our boy to be civilized, open-minded, and inclusive. To know that the thoughtful and sensitive man is always superior to the one who communicates with his testosterone as an amplifier. When his growing body is flooded with hormones and muscle spurts that make him want to be loud, brutish, and oversexual, we shove him back toward childhood and exorcise his violent inclinations with cartoons, Funko Pop collectibles, comics, and video games. If he still feels restless, we are the first subscribers to his video-blog, where he recites his poetry, all written deliberately without punctuation.

We've considerably changed our vision of what used to be considered "the ideal boy."

Ascott Robert Hope Moncrieff, a lifelong schoolmaster of boys, described the best sort of Victorian boy in his 1886 *A Book About Boys.*

> *I like the happy, healthy, unsophisticated boy, who is a boy, and not a young gentleman; active, restless, generous, brave, truthful, simple, and pure-minded, who thinks it half a pleasure to bear pain without crying, climbs trees, tears his trousers, has frequent tumbles, bumps, and bruises, and comes home now and then splashed over with mud.*

Do you miss the idea of the scrappy little boy, covered in mud and mischief? The strong teen boy, navigating even the most awkward years with confidence and chivalry? You should. Just because society has changed doesn't mean a boy's biology has. It's your job, Mother, to funnel that healthy animalistic nature into something noble. Herald the return of the Masculine Boy.

Q: I take issue with your narrow definition of masculinity, your insistence upon it, and your degradation of bringing up a son gently.

A: I know. And I, in turn, am shocked at your veneration of methods that encourage weakness and punish natural biological impulses. Now, we've ticked those boxes. Shall we continue? Do you want to know how Victorians set about creating a boy of honor, strength, and vitality?

Q: Yes, but it's morbid curiosity at this point.

A: Good enough! First, of course, is to take the prenatal measures we discussed in earlier chapters. Expose the fetus to a good balance of manly influences while in utero—fine cigar smoke, nourishing well-aged whiskey, and the witnessing of blood shed in an honorable and valiant manner, as Napoleon's mother did—all excellent ways to prepare your little man. But remember, he is to be your little man. After the first year of his life, he is no longer your baby doll.

Moncrieff has dealt with those boys. And they squick him out: "I don't think much of your gentlemanly, neat boys, and I abominate your pretty, effeminate boys, and I have not so much faith as some people in even your good, clever boys, who are always at the head of their classes, and never do anything naughty, except when it is not found out."

The earliest thing you can do for the health of your son, once he no longer depends upon your robust Guinness-infused milk, is back off, Mama. Moncrieff described the very worst of the boys he was inclined to headmaster during his career.

"I'm Mama's special, special boy, hehhhh."

> *Mammas' Darlings.—A large and increasing class… their degradation is often caused by circumstances over which neither they, nor the wisest of writers and teachers, have any control, viz., fond and foolish mothers, who will make them wear comforters and galoshes, and keep them in the house when it is cold, and encourage them to cry when they are hurt.*

The only freedom from suffering is the strength to go through it. Comfort your boy at every turn, remove the edges from his life, and watch him spend the rest of his days getting bruised by whatever touches him.

Q: But I love my boys. Surely a little coddling won't hurt?

A: Won't hurt? See, this is why it took so long for women to get the vote. We too often make the mistake of thinking with our squishy mother-hearts and not our heads. Won't hurt? Well, let's consult Mr. John Stevens Cabot Abbott, who published *The Mother at Home, or The Principles of Maternal Duty, Familiarly Illustrated.* Cabot Abbott was only in his midtwenties when he wrote his treatise of "maternal duties," but don't think his youth, his lack of study, or his not being a mother in any way lessened his ability to correct bad mothering. Because he still had *eyes.* And was therefore qualified to tell you and every other mother smart enough to listen how you were failing at your only purpose on this earth. Here he tells the story of a woman who spoiled her only son with indulgences and affection.

> *At the death of his father, the poor woman was left at the mercy of this vile boy. One day, infuriated with his mother, he set fire to her house, and it was burned to the ground, with all its contents, and she was left in the extremest state of poverty. He was imprisoned, and, in his cell, he became a maniac, and dug out his own eyes. He now lies in perpetual darkness, confined by the stone walls, and grated bars of his dungeon, an infuriated madman.*

Gouged out his own eyes after burning his mother's house down. All because Mother couldn't withhold that extra slice of cake, couldn't stand firm on bedtime. How's that for "not hurting"?

Q: I think you're being dramatic again.

A: Of course, being an overaffectionate mother doesn't always end with fire and blood and blindness. But it does end *badly.* If

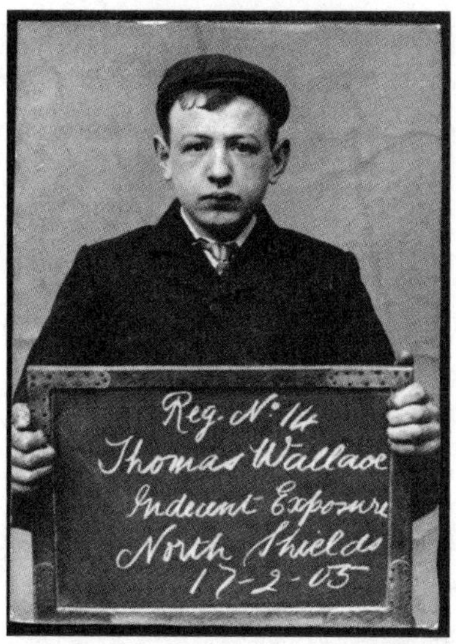

The coddled boy: Thomas Wallace was only eighteen in this mugshot. Though he'd been caught exposing himself to girls on three separate occasions, his delusional mother testified that he was "a kind, hard-working, well disposed lad."

coddling sons *doesn't* make them violent madmen, it most certainly weakens them. In fact, a boyish insult, used by the full-grown man Pye Henry Chavasse in his 1872 book on "the mental culture and training of a child," stems from that very word: the "mollycoddle," or as Chavasse put it:

> *Mollet-coddle.—A child should be encouraged to be manly and not be made a mollet coddle. Some boys are brought up more like girls than boys—being tied to their mother's apron-strings: such boys are deeply to be pitied, and are quite unfitted for the rough world they will have to struggle in.*

Chavasse has another good name for weak feminine boys, since classics like *sissy, wuss, pantywaist,* and *wimp* weren't in vogue yet. He has quite a few, as only a boy named Pye would have to stockpile. This one is Shakespearean!

> *Milk Sop.—A child who is brought up a milksop is not well fitted for this rough world of ours...he should be brought up rather hardily, than otherwise; he should be made to rough it; to live on plain, simple fare; and to be more than half his time in the open air.*

That's right. A hardy boy should feel the cold on his shoes, the growl for porridge in his lean belly, and the wind whipping right up his tiny pretty dress.

Albert Einstein, age three. In a dress and is already better at math than you.

Q: I wish you'd pick an insanely bigoted perspective and stick with it. Dresses? I put my boy in dresses? And it won't damage his little man-psyche?

A: You mean like it damaged *these* poor children? Oh wait, I'm sorry. I meant to display pictures of transvestite serial killers here but I somehow mixed them up with the ones of boys who grew up to alter the course of history through their strength and intelligence.

The little-boys-wearing-dresses thing... It wasn't really a dress. It was "this small human poops himself daily, changes clothing size monthly, and the soft cotton stretch-neck snap-crotch onesie with his mom's favorite 1980s punk band emblazoned on the

Franklin D. Roosevelt, 1885. If polio and Hitler weren't going to stop him from being the president to hold the longest term in office, that dress and haircut sure weren't gonna either.

front doesn't exist yet" garment. (Thankfully, neither did the ones that say "Bad Mother-Sucker" or "Made in Vachina.")

Smocks are easy to sew, easy to flip up for a diaper change, and allow room to grow. A toddler's bathroom and table habits, as well as their tendency to fall a lot, account for the predominance of white in baby and toddler smocks. They were filthy little creatures, bless them. Bleaching made white easiest to clean. But for fancier occasions, a boy needed a more impressive frock.

In an 1895 edition of the parenting periodical *Babyhood; The Mother's Nursery Guide,* mothers wrote letters to the editor in answer to the question of what a baby boy should wear. A mother from Hackensack, New Jersey, described the masculine touches that made her toddler's ensemble fit for a boy:

> *This little boy is sturdy and well grown for two years of age, and wears little dresses made of pique [heavy-weave cotton] and other washable materials of heavy weight. The dresses are all in one piece, buttoned in the back. The waist part is perfectly plain, with a neat turn-down collar, and the sleeves are full and gathered into a plain turned-over cuff. The skirt part is pleated and sewed to the waist, and where the two parts join, the little boy wears a belt, either of russet leather or of the dress material stiffened.... There is no trimming of any kind; the dresses are easily washed, and their small wearer, in spite of baby chubbiness, looks what he is—a boy.*

Other mothers made minor variations, replacing white pique with flannel in colder weather or using the term "kilt" instead of skirt, and, yes, there were a few who couldn't help embroidering flowers and using pearly buttons on their boy's pretty dresses. But most mothers agreed that a simple design was best, made of sturdy cloth that was easy to remove and wash, with tidy lines and belts to cinch the most adjustable garment in history.

Q: Actually, I'm not too surprised about the dress. Gender is a construct. HEY! Did you know that one hundred years ago pink used to be a BOY'S color and blue was for GIR—?

A: NO. No, no, no. Don't be that person. The one at the baby shower who must vomit this enlightenment over the squeals of joy that erupt when the pregnant mother cuts into the pink sponge of the Reveal Cake. Is gender completely a social construct? A great question to pose in your next blog post. But an inappropriate smug-bomb to drop in a room full of women rallying a lady about to sacrifice her body and her sleep and her life as she knows it for

"George, old man! I say, that's a handsome cream pique you're wearing. I myself prefer flannel."

the love of a baby. A woman who, no matter how feminist she is, is easing herself through Braxton-Hicks at this very moment with comforting pictures of how frickin' adorable her daughter's first Easter dress and bonnet are going to be.

Let them have this, Comrade Buzzkill.

Besides. You're wrong about the colors.

The basis for the twenty-first century's most obnoxious baby shower fake fun fact seems to have been a handful of department store circulars and ladies' magazines from the early twentieth century. The psychologist Marco Del Giudice published a paper trying to locate the source of "pink-blue reversal" (PBR), the theory that up until one hundred years ago these colors represented the opposite genders they do now. He was able to track down four, *four,* primary source mentions from old magazines, fashion advice all, not documentation of people actually using these colors in their reversed manner. He then compared those four mentions to a database of over five million books published between 1800 and 2000 for all permutations of the terms "pink for girls" and "blue for boys."

Giudice concluded: "This massive book database contains no trace of the alleged pink-blue reversal; on the contrary, the results show remarkable consistency in gender coding over time in both the US and the UK, starting from the late nineteenth century and continuing throughout the twentieth century."

Q: Mm. Maybe. All the photos of the era are black-and-white, so we'll never know for sure.

A: Oh, you stubborn gender-bender. Dig out that old three-hundred-dollar, seven-hundred-page history of art textbook you had to buy in college and have been lugging around ever since, on pure principle that something that expensive must be useful. Look at the last few centuries of children in paintings. Rich children in portraiture, poor children sketched by starving artists. Find me the boy in manly pink. Girls in blue, sure; blue is as gender neutral as the sky. And sure...you'll find boys in flossy shades of brown that have a reddish tinge, you'll find them dressed in silks and velvets, embroidered with flowers that might even have a drop or two of coral in them, but you will not find a true pink. And if you're *still* not convinced, consult the actual clothing itself, as kept by the many museums that have collected children's wear over the centuries. You'll find red and even purple that has faded, since dyes of previous centuries were not as adherent, but a peek inside a seam not exposed to sun and wear will show you the intended hue. He might be wearing a dress...*but it won't be pink!*

Q: Okay! Aside from dressing him in not-pink dresses, what else can I do to shape my son into a strong but kind young man?

A: See, this *neediness* of yours, this is what makes boys grow up into monsters. Give him space, Mother, that's what you do! Nature has equipped your son with an animalistic nature for a reason. Your job is to direct it, temper it, but not squash it. (Save the squashing for your daughters.)

He will need discipline, fairly and consistently delivered. Says Cabot Abbott, "If, you cannot summon resolution to punish your child when disobedient; if you do not curb his passions; if you do not bring him to entire and willing subjection to your authority; you must expect that he will be your curse. In all probability, he will despise you for your weakness."

But not the same kind of discipline as you give your daughter. Because your daughter wasn't created by God to, and I quote the deity Himself, "rule over the fish of the sea and over the birds of the sky and over the cattle and over all the earth, and over every creeping thing that creeps on the earth" (Gen. 1:26).

World domination, that is literally Man's job. And it ain't a job for no mamma's darling, mollycoddled milksop. Lydia Howard Sigourney explains in 1838's *Letters to Mothers,*

> *Let [mothers] ever keep in view, the different spheres of action allotted to the sexes. What they blame as obstinacy, may be but that firmness, and fixedness of purpose, which will hereafter be needed to overcome the obstacles of their adventurous course. Perhaps, it is hardly to be expected that they should be reduced to the full degree of feminine subordination.*

So, what *you* see as being an obstinate little turd is actually your son claiming his natural birthright. The key for you, Mother dear, is to act quick, while he is young. He won't tolerate your feminine goosiness for long, says Sigourney; it's an unnatural relationship: "By the constitution of society, he must be earlier removed from the influence of home, than his pliant sister, and by the innate consciousness of being born to bear rule, will sooner revolt from the authority of woman."

Your job, while he is still small, is to "enthrone yourself" in his heart. Teach him to submit to your will out of devotion and love. As a queen is defended by her generals, in turn they dine at her table and reap her benevolence. If she's angry with them for snagging a piece of cake…or a few villages that she was saving for a special occasion, she doesn't shriek and squawk and paddle their bottoms in front of the whole court. She either punishes them by withdrawing her benevolent affection, or by execution (telling Father when he gets home). That is to be your relationship to your son.

"I can SO dominate Earth! Just first kiss my boo-boo."

Q: He's not a general! I don't want him brawling and fighting! Violence never solved anything.

A: Violence never solved...Lord give me strength. Madam, *violence solved Hitler*. He didn't surrender the Third Reich and commit suicide because the Allied Forces had *gently discussed* their way into Berlin. No, they'd laid waste to it, because they had to. Violence has solved slavery. Violence has solved oppression. Violence has solved...angry bears! Violence causes problems, yes, and that's not going to change. So it's fitting that sometimes only violence can fix them. Mothers of old understood that. You might think, as Margaret Sangster put it in "Shall Your Boy Fight?," that it is noble for your son to meet violence with peace, but if he looks weak to everyone else, he will never know actual peace. She says:

"My queen has refused me ice cream for my insolence. I shall endeavor to regain her favor."

> *A boy who is known to be ready in the art of self-defense is not often molested by the bully, the latter being generally a coward. A mother hates to see her little man of ten disfigured by a black eye, though there are many worse things that may come to him, and she should not too hastily condemn him if he stand up for himself at need in a fair fight.*

The schoolyard fight is a microcosm of the world.

> *Our boys are preparing for life in the larger world. We want them to be morally and physically fit for the conflict. In settling for ourselves the question, Shall the*

Shall your boy fight?

> *small boy fight, or shall he refrain from fighting? we must think of his future. The one thing he cannot do is to run away. He must not show the white feather. If he declines a fight, he must be strong enough to show in other ways that he does it through no lack of courage.*

Q: Speaking of schoolyards and fights, should I send my son away to school? I want him to have the finest education, but I've heard horrible things happen at boys' schools.

A: You want to know if your boy is in danger of becoming someone's fag, right?

Q: N…no, not like that…I mean…I'll support him no matter what his orientation, but…

A: Because you *should* be worrying about what will happen if he *doesn't* behave like a proper fag. A well-managed system of faggery is a good way to avoid unneeded violence.

Ostensibly, the fagging system in British schools prevented this sort of bullying. Or at least reduced it to acceptable standards of the day.

Q: I don't think you're allowed to say "fag" that many times.

A: Pish. It's a rude word today, but it wasn't always so! Edmund Routledge published "Recollections of an Old Boy" in an 1869 edition of *Every Boy's Annual* that detailed the fagging system at Victorian boys' schools.

> *The arrangement was somewhat after this fashion. The sixth form, or prefects, were allowed so many fags; the fifth form so many; the fourth form could neither fag or be fagged; and all the rest of the school were liable to be fagged.*
>
> *It was determined that fagging should go by seniority, and not by brute strength. This plan succeeded*

> *admirably. Everybody liked it except the third-form bullies. The little fellows were delighted.*

You've never seen that word used as so many parts of speech in one paragraph, have you? Well, English is a thriving language.

Granted, Americans are and were less keen to embrace fagging; our macho bravado makes our boys think they're too good to heat up another boy's sausage.

Q: Nice. Subtle.

A: In fact, American derision accounts for "fag" becoming a term intended to be sexual and demeaning.

But in England, where classicism was an inculcated tradition, fagging was a matter of course. "To fag" for another boy was to be his manservant, shine his shoes and fetch him treats. This is probably a slang corruption of the word *fatigue,* mixed with an interpretation of *flag* as it was used for many hundreds of years to mean "running out of energy." Or course you might also want to include *faggot,* referring to the small branches that were often used to flog misbehaving boys—that seems to fit in there...somewhere—as in, "My interest in shining my own boot is beginning to *flag.* I find it *fatiguing* work. But I'm one of the oldest boys in the school and shall use my seniority to have my *fag,* a younger, weaker boy, do this tiring, ungratifying *fagging* work instead. If he doesn't do it properly I'll give him such a *fagging* with my bundle of birch *faggots* because...he...there was...he *fagged* out in the end."

I'm sorry, I'm getting tangled.

It's...it's not a straight etymological line. English is thriving but it is also a greedy and ill-mannered little language and when you mix it with schoolboys and spankings, everything just goes sideways.

Q: That's okay. I'm caught up now on fa— on that system. In fact, we could actually completely move on if you'd like.

A: Shhh. It's important to understand that this sort of servitude would have been a comfortable concept to boys wealthy enough to attend English boarding schools. Their fathers would have had butlers and valets to aid them in their day-to-day living; why shouldn't a growing boy procure his own servants? And this was not, writes the Old Boy, meant to be a form of bullying, but a way to prevent it.

> *I will still venture to assert that the non-fagging system encouraged bullying instead of stopping it. Mothers have an idea that fags are bullied by their boy-masters. This is a great mistake. Masters, as a rule, expect their fags to fag for them, and in turn protect them from being bullied.*

Q: Like...like in all those horrible prison movies? Because that sounds just like what stronger inmates do to weaker ones in all the prison movies—

A: Ehh ehh ehh...I said "Shhh," dear. Let the Old Boy continue.

> *I was at Marlborough both in the fagging and non-fagging days, and I pronounce entirely in favour of the former system. When there is no organized plan for fagging, the biggest and strongest boys—very frequently those incorrigibly idle, dull, and stupid fellows who stick in the third form for everlasting—fag the whole school.*

So hep hep for the good old fags! When left to their own devices, civilized boys needed no coddling. They established their own fiefdoms and hierarchies, where all benefited.

Of course, not all parents believed the hierarchies of public school a healthy environment for boys. (By the way, when British writers say "public school," they mean "private school," as in a boarding school the parent pays for. When they say "college" they mean "high school." When they say "sixth form"...I don't know. I think it means you've earned full rights to drink butter beer in Hogsmeade with Ron and Hermione and cast low-level enchantments without permission from the Ministry of Magic. The English. Pfft. Honestly, just because a language is named after your civilization doesn't entitle you to use it however you wish.)

Some saw the boys' school as a dangerous playground for humanity's most vicious, including Lydia Howard Sigourney, who wrote: "I compare, the sending a boy to a publick school, or college, says a judicious writer, to the act of the Scythian mothers, who threw their new-born children into the sea: the greater part, were of course, drowned, but the few who escaped with life, were uncommonly strong and vigorous."

Hmm. Now...that's what the mother of a sinker kid would say. Something we might call, in any century, loser talk. No. You are forewarned by reading this book, and you are going to be the mother of one of the survivors. Toss him in. If you've done your job right, he's going to be just fine.

Q: But...isn't there a high occurrence of...improper intimacies... between boys at these schools?

A: Yes! A lot!

Q: Shouldn't it be stopped?

A: I suppose. I'd also like to stop lightning from striking at inopportune times and places and igniting flash fires. But lightning, like

an adolescent boy's sexual development, is simply too powerful a force to completely contain.

Adolescent boys have brains, but they are so very underdeveloped. Except for the part that tells them *Orgasms are terrific and you ought to have lots!* That part of the brain is possibly the most active it will ever be at the exact same time Victorians removed most female contact from wealthy boys. It was generally understood that some boys would just have to…make do with what they had. Or what the boy sleeping in the same bed with them had.

That sort of experimentation was present, fairly expected, and not talked about for most of the nineteenth century. And probably every century. But around the 1880s, there developed the relatively fresh idea that homosexuality was a *psychological* illness, not a naughty diversion for boys at bedtime nor the desperate act of a sex-starved shanghaied-ship-bound swabbie. Boys' boarding schools figured prominently in the new psychologists' attempts to decode what made a man homo- or heterosexual.

When describing homosexual patients, doctors always noted the parentage of the man in question. Without fail, the natural-born, or *congenital,* homosexual had deviant parents. Criminals, madmen, whores, thieves, actors, artists. All the reprobates of society were capable of spawning congenital (since birth) homosexuals.

There was a far more interesting and genial term for the homosexual man in this century, a *Uranian,* coined by an early crusader of the idea that homosexuals were not only decent, but uniquely gifted people, Karl Ulrichs. He took the word *Uranian,* or *Urning,* from...ah...Uranus.

Q: Oh, I'm sorry. Could you repeat that?

A: No.

Q: No, no, you were saying? Uranus is responsible for homosexuality in men?

A: No, YOUR anus...is...no. I shan't stoop. With a filthy mind and sass-mouth like that it's no wonder you're having trouble raising decent children. All right, yes, it is an unfortunate coincidence, but he had his reasons! First of all, I'm sure it's not as punny in the original German. Second, Uranus was a Greek god, and when his mother-wife got mad at him she had their son-brother cut off his testicles and cast them into the sea, where one of them (the testicles) sprouted Aphrodite, Goddess of Love! *Aphrodite Urania* (daughter of Uranus), to be more specific. We take the last part of Aphrodite's name and we get a *Uranian:* a person with a female psyche born into a male body! See? It's actually very clever and rather sweet. If you can just not focus on the imagery of giant severed testi-

Uranus's biggest mistake here was waiting to see how this would play out.

cles falling from the sky in a blood storm and bouncing atop a roiling sea from which somehow, perhaps with much screaming and ripping flesh, escapes a fully formed sex goddess. If you can do that, it's hardly terrifying at all. As psychology gained a foothold in the scientific world, those who studied homosexuals identified a second kind of "sexual invert." The *non*-congenital homosexual. The man who had no inborn predisposition to the pleasures of Uranus (oh, shut *up!*), but had "acquired" homosexuality. These men were born heterosexual, but through exposure and environment in their youth, had decided homosexuality was just more kicky.

Q: And it was overexposure to other boys that spawned this "acquired" inversion?

A: Often, yes. By the end of the nineteenth century it became a point of contention that the most common way for boys to contract noncongenital Uranianism was all-boy boarding schools.

Havelock Ellis wrote in his 1901 *Studies in the Psychology of Sex*,

> *The school is undoubtedly the great breeding-place of artificial homosexuality among the general population. Its influence in this respect may have been overestimated, but it is undoubtedly large. It is very unfortunate that school-authorities do their best to ignore and conceal the facts. We probably have to recognize that the only way to render such manifestations wholesome, as well as to prepare for the relationships of later life, is to insure the adoption, so far as possible, of the methods of co-education of the sexes.*

Q: For the record, I'm totally fine with my son being gay. I think I would have been in Victorian times, too.

A: Of course you would have! You'd have worn blue jeans, voted for increased public services, been Harriet Tubman's bestie, and driven cars that hadn't been invented yet too! Oh! Who needs cars when you could have just flown everywhere on the updraft of your superior social consciousness?

You don't know how you would have felt. The first rule of loving history is that you can never judge it by the standards of today. If you thought your son was attracted to other men, you would have struggled much harder in Victorian times, because nearly all of society would have been against the both of you. At the very least, you would have wished to spare your child the pain of being so separate, so maligned.

In which case I would have comforted you by bringing forth the few examples of forward thought on the subject. Be proud that you've contributed a Uranian to this world. After all, on the whole, they're reputed to be a very tidy and productive people! Albert

Moll, writing *The Sexual Life of the Child* in 1912, enumerates the professions homosexuals often seek to fill, and they are *fabulous.*

> *The homosexual ladies' tailor, the music-hall artiste who makes a specialty of feminine impersonations, the ladies' hairdresser, and others in like occupations, will often tell us that the choice of their trade or profession was made while they were still children. In this connexion, I may also refer to the sexual life of Catholic priests. It is certain that some of these exhibit homosexual tendencies.*

So you may have contributed an artist to the world! Or maybe even a...Catholic priest. Which is a high calling and quite respectable! I mean, a bit more...complicated, maybe...but you know what? If *your* Uranian son wants to be a priest, you raise him to be the best darn priest in the diocese and let God worry about his (legal, between consenting adults) sexual preference. A well-raised boy of any predilection can be virtuous and celibate if he believes God so desires it.

Q: I *do* like what my son did with my hair for our Mother's Day formal, but I still want grandchildren. Isn't there *any* available cure for sexual inversion?

A: Oh, don't worry about grandchildren. Many homosexual men, perhaps most who lived in the Victorian era, preferred the status and comfort of a home and family. They would marry women and have babies all the time. Some still do, though now the options for Uranians to have children are far more varied. As for a cure...oh, no, I'm sorry. Really, they tried. They tried just everything.

The late nineteenth century saw the introduction and quick

demise of every type of "cure" possible for male homosexuality. Hypnosis was very popular for a while, early psychoanalysts building on Freud's teachings to draw out a man's early love for his mother and expand it to all womankind, which was the current belief on how heterosexuality was formed. But the recidivism was nearly 100 percent.

Q: Hmm. Maybe because sex and your mom are not as sexy a combination as Freud supposed.

A: Agreed. Moll himself supported an "association bridge" technique wherein a homosexual man unable to perform sexually with his wife "read homosexual literature and contemplated male figures. Becoming greatly excited he went into his wife's room and succeeded for the first time in coitus." It was Moll's theory that though homosexual thoughts got the party swinging, since the climax of the event would be heterosexual, the inverted man would learn to associate orgasms and sex with his wife. That didn't work. Men just realized they could manage to have depressing sex with women if they thought about men while doing it.

Some doctors recommended an "uneventful, hardening life" with spare diet and hard work regimens, until it was realized that method bore great resemblance to prison life: a place not known for its lack of homosexual encounters.

Isolation in colonies was considered, but was dismissed for being too cruel and unnecessary, as most homosexuals were not dangerous and in fact contributed to society. Though some asked to be isolated, as a measure to protect others. At least one man, described in a study by the nineteenth-century German sexologist Magnus Hirschfeld, submitted to it voluntarily. He had "been interned as a criminal lunatic for twenty years and at his own request. He occupies a fine room, supplied with books and pursues philosophical studies. His impulses are entirely toward boys who have just passed puberty. He expected to end his life there."

Other homosexuals were so desperate they sought the "scorched earth" cure, castration (not the chemical kind—the Uranus kind), sometimes followed by emasculation.

Q: Oh, God, that's heartbreaking. Those poor men.

A: And sadly ineffective. Says Leon Pierce Clark in *A Critical Digest of Some of the Newer Work Upon Homosexuality in Man and Woman,* it still did not make men stop desiring their own sex. Says Clark,

Even after years of living the prescribed "uneventful, hardening life," Matvey and Stiven had to conclude they still felt pretty gay.

> *Homosexuals have asked for castration and it has been advocated but this would seem highly illogical and experience shows that to remove the testicles of a homosexual aggravates his state. As it has been done only in extreme cases the impulses were not increased but remained the same. The additional emasculation weakened the patient's will and made him, if possible, more of a menace than he was at first.*

The "menace" implied in this context was not the fact of homosexuality, but men who abused unwilling partners.

The bottom line seeming to be, your Uranian is yours to keep. He (and his parents) may not like it, but for him, it appears to be a natural state.

Or, more eloquently put by the poet John Addington Symonds, saying of his own homosexuality in an 1897 edition of Havelock Ellis's *Sexual Inversion:*

> *I cannot regard my sexual feelings as unnatural or abnormal, since they have disclosed themselves so perfectly naturally and spontaneously within me. With regard to the morality of this complex subject, my feeling is that it is the same as should prevail in love between man and woman—namely, that no bodily satisfaction should be sought at the cost of another person's distress or degradation. I am sure that this kind of love is, notwithstanding the physical difficulties that attend it, as deeply stirring and ennobling as the other kind.*

John Addington Symonds.

Besides, our goal is masculinity. It doesn't matter if you need to make your peace with the fact that your grandchildren will be furry and want bacon-flavored plastic for Christmas, or that your son wants to kiss other boys. What matters is that he has the strength of mind and body to also punch them if he needs to.

Q: All right. The bottom line is I *do* want a strong, bold, and happy boy. I guess that means masculine. But I don't want an entitled little dude-bro jerk. How can I have one and not the other?

PHYSICAL STRENGTH v. INTELLECT.

Tom (who has been "shut up" by the Crichton-like accomplishments of his cousin Augustus). "I TAN'T SING, AND I TAN'T 'PEAK FRENSS—BUT I TAN PUNSS YOUR 'ED!"

"I can't sing, I can't speak French, but I can punch your head!"

A: And here will be the test of your parenting. To raise a man of perfect masculinity, not a mama's boy, without creating a cruel and animalistic brute. But, loving Mother, though you can and should expect your boy to shun you as he grows, these precious early years are when you unleash your secret weapon. You have a woman's heart. And many Victorians were of the opinion that no man could be complete without absorbing a bit of it into his own.

Charles Benjamin Tayler was a country parson who'd lost his own mother in childhood. In 1822 he published *May You Like It, by a Country Curate,* which contains the best advice for accomplishing your mission. And it came, from all places, from a father. Said Tayler:

> *My father was anxious to make me manly and courageous. "I cannot bear," he would say, "to see a weak effeminate boy; ill health can be the only excuse for it. I would have you fear no one but God. But remember, my dear Charles, there is a great difference between being effeminate, and possessing many of those gentle and humble graces, which are more peculiarly present in the character of the best women; and are called therefore feminine. Many of these were displayed in the conduct of our Saviour, and all truly good and noble men have possessed the most gentle hearts. To be effeminate, is to act like a weak silly woman; to be almost feminine in some things, is to act with the purity, and gentleness, and humanity, of a virtuous woman.*

There's no denying how tricky a balancing act it is to build a masculine boy. He must be tough, stubborn, and feminine without being effeminate. Because until humans have finished their evolution into genderless light beams of telepathy, men and women will have different concerns, problems, and demands. Plus, men are ordained by God to subjugate the earth to their will. Which is a big job. Following the robust Victorian standard, it is your job to prepare your son for that, without getting in his way.

8

How May I Distinguish Healthful Amusements My Child Might Engage in from Those That Are Satan Disguised in the Raiment of Light and Joy?

On Appropriate Recreations for Children

The first necessity in arranging safe and uplifting amusement for your Victorian child is to understand that almost no amusement is safe and uplifting. Sin lurks everywhere, in the most enticing, or innocent, of places.

To wit: In 1915, Fred F. McClure measured the amount of sin in Kansas City and presented his findings in *Christianity and Amusements,* by Richard Henry Edwards.

Motion Picture Shows	79	per	cent	good
Theatres	72	"	"	"
Dance Halls	23.1	"	"	"
River Excursion Boats	7.7	"	"	"
Pool Halls	46.2	"	"	"
Skating Rinks	74.1	"	"	"
Penny Arcades	38.5	"	"	"
Shows—"Men Only"	0	"	"	"
Shooting Galleries	84.7	"	"	"
Bowling Alleys	77.1	"	"	"
Amusement Parks	71.1	"	"	"

Percentage of goodness (as opposed to sinfulness) in common Kansas City amusements.

Please note: "Medical museums, social clubs, wine gardens, chop suey restaurants, and saloons are not graded. They would undoubtedly lower the average of good, wholesome recreation."

McClure was then able to provide the following conclusions: "The totals show traditionally 'wholesome' amusements are actually 68 per cent wholesome; they are 32 per cent loathsome. The 32 per cent consists of 'intemperance, obscenity, suggestions of crime, dissipation, late hours, representing an expenditure of $1,923,211.99.'"

Q: Chop suey restaurants? Dissipation? How could he possibly measure wholesomeness of museums and Chinese restaurants, much less find them wanting?

A: I don't know, I'm not a scientist. I don't think he was either, but, look, he used math. So there you have it. The world then, as now, was steeped in the raw sewage of unmonitored pleasures for youth. It is our duty as parents to select amusement for our children that is edifying, wholesome, and free of MSG.

As George Sumner Weaver wrote in 1868's *Hopes and Helps for the Young of Both Sexes,*

> *Amusements have dissipated [a child's] mind, stolen his heart, corrupted his manners and morals, eaten up his earnings, made him the child of folly, and the dupe of an insatiable desire for a life of giddiness. The more exciting any amusement is, the more dangerous it is. I say dangerous, yes, dangerous—that is the word. It is truly so.*

"Fun," Mother dear, stands for "fool's unrighteous nonsense" if not attended to with the greatest of severity and solemnity.

Q: All right, fair enough. I agree that there are many things my children enjoy that aren't good for them. What sort of entertainments *were* suitable for Victorian children?

A: Much depends on age and gender. But all amusements must have purpose. Outdoor play was considered a very noble undertaking, necessary to help children who lived in an increasingly urban world partake of the fresh air, physical movement, and sunshine so necessary to health.

"Whatever you do, don't get that suit wet. You'll sink like a stone."

There were a handful of activities both genders could engage in together. Everyone could play a little lawn tennis or croquet. Wading into the ocean dressed in full woolen mourning garb was permitted to both sexes. Most outdoor sports were intended for boys alone.

Q: Wait! No, stop. I appreciate Victorian values, but I also believe boys and girls are equal in their need for challenging physical play and that a girl can and should do anything a boy does.

A: Then you in no way appreciate Victorian values. Boys were trained by their games to become tough and clever under fire. Girls were being trained in patience and piety to balance their masculine counterparts. Our good German doctor Heinrich Hoffmann (often listed as "Henry" Hoffmann, depending on whom we were at war with) can illustrate the dangers of intergender play better than anyone. Meet "Romping Polly."

Polly was warned not to play with the boys by her auntie, who said:

Do try to be more steady.
I know that you will often see
Rude boys push, drive, and hurry;
But little girls should never be
All in a heat and flurry.

Polly didn't listen. She went out to play with the boys, but, being a delicate female, fell and broke her leg. Popped that sucker clean off, left her little brother wandering around the yard holding it.

And then was horribly crippled and died slowly.

Q: …

A: Stop face-palming, dear. It's terrible for your complexion. We'll explore girls' amusements in a moment. Now. Games for boys!

For organized sports, both baseball and basketball made their debut toward the end of the nineteenth century, though they were slow to take hold. The "organized" aspect was a challenge to children in a world with few parks, no standardized schedules, and limited transportation. Not to mention, the necessary equipment, even if only a simple ball and bat, was hard to come by. An exception is soccer, which could be played with anything remotely resembling a ball. Variations of soccer have been found by archaeologists the world over, from nearly every time and culture.

Q: Hey, quick question. How come the rest of the world calls soccer football, and what do they call *actual* football?

A: They call it American football. We Americans call it football because we changed it so much that we couldn't call it rugby anymore, which in turn had become so different from the nineteenth-century version of itself that it couldn't be called by its original name, which was football, and both had to be differentiated from the original ball-kicking game we now call soccer.

Q: Oh. I see.

A: Oh, please. No, you don't. *No one does.* That's not even taking into account all the other versions of "football" that different nations claim as their own. But as for American football, its origins are dimly brought to light in an 1883 volume of the

"Sockyfootruggeryball" was very popular among colleges of the late nineteenth century.

periodical *Young England,* where the Reverend Thomas Keyworth writes an article painstakingly explaining the difference between "the two kinds of football." The first kind was favored by the men attending Rugby College in England, so it became the rugby style, which involves less padded, muddy, sexy young men in tiny shorts and wool sweaters brawling over a ball that resembles a lumpy ham. The other way to play was to follow rules set forth by some guys at a pub who called themselves the Football Association. This was less handsy and more kicky. So, you either played rugby style or "Soc" ("Association") style. Or, "rugger versus socker" styles.

American Ivy League schools had rugby football *and* Association football clubs. Over the decades, the schools begin refining the rules of rugby until it no longer fit under that heading, so it was just "football."

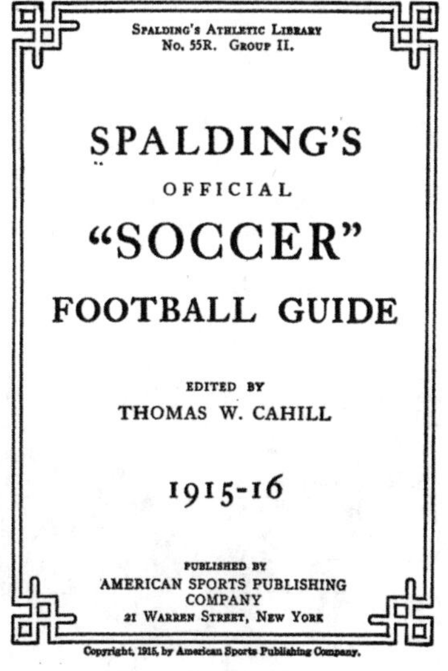
Spalding's Athletic Library
No. 55R. Group II.

SPALDING'S
OFFICIAL
"SOCCER"
FOOTBALL GUIDE

EDITED BY
THOMAS W. CAHILL

1915-16

PUBLISHED BY
AMERICAN SPORTS PUBLISHING
COMPANY
21 Warren Street, New York

Copyright, 1915, by American Sports Publishing Company.

A historic match held by the Carlisle Indian School, a college meant to train Native Americans for skilled labor, helped draw even more interest to the sport when they played Harvard in an exhibition match and first used some of the favored guerrilla tactics of the game, like the false pass-off. They nearly tied the far more practiced men of Harvard.

Association football, "soccer," never gained the passionate following in America that the rest of the world held for it, perhaps, as suggested by Virgil C. Aldrich in an article entitled "A Theory of Ball-Play," published in an 1879 edition of the *Psychological Review,* because Americans care less about "aerial play" and truly enjoy the displays of "power and deception" that "are the two fundamentals of American football."

Q: That's rather small-minded and insult—

A: *USA! USA! USA!* Own it, honey.

Q: Fine. What about nonorganized sports? What sort of games will help build my child's character?

A: Ah! Now the real fun begins! Throw out the iPad and cancel the noncompetitive fun runs, Mother! We're going to teach your children strength and cunning! (Do not throw out the ice compresses, bandages, or antiseptic ointments, however. You're going to need *a lot* of those.) Here are some popular amusements set forth in the Reverend John George Wood's 1891 book *The Boy's Modern Playmate: A Book of Sports, Games, and Pastimes.* (As his title tells you, these are, of course, intended only for boys.)

Jingling

First pen and blindfold your children. Except for the one you tie a bell to. He is the Jingler! And his job is to escape the pen without being wrestled down by his blind companions, all while constantly jingling his bell.

Says Wood,

JINGLING.

> *There is positively no end to the fun that may be got out of the game: a good jingler will lead the blind men into all sorts of scrapes, of course without compromising himself—into each other's arms, over the ropes, or over some luckless companion who has come to grief in labouring after the jingler, or a hundred other devices equally effective and amusing.*

The winner is whoever pins the Jingler down in the mud, or the Jingler himself, if he escapes after a set time limit without being caught.

But for real fun you'll need an angry pig and some buggy whips.

Q: Obviously. I'm always thinking how those exact objects would liven up the office.

A: Because, as Wood explains,

> *A somewhat similar though rougher game is played in some parts of the country. A pig is substituted for the*

jingler, and the blind men are all armed with cart-whips. He who hits the pig gets him.

At first the players are very cautious and try to find out the pig before they strike; but they soon find that does not pay, and begin slashing about recklessly right and left, and the fun gets fast and furious: their heads and faces are protected from the blows, but the way they belabour each other, especially about the legs, is enough to make the spectator die with laughter.

This version of jingling is superior because in many cases the Pig Smacker then gets to eat the pig! Worth a bit of flayed skin, I'd say!

Q: I'm sorry...I actually didn't get much past the "pen and blindfolding" part. Anything without bondage?

A: Come now, Mater! You're already practicing bondage if you keep a boy tied to your apron strings! But perhaps you'd rather something with a bit more mobility? Something like Sling the Monkey or Baste the Bear.

Sling the Monkey

First, you'll need a good strong tree from which to hang your child. Or, if shipboard, the masting will work quite well. The treed child is "the Monkey." Ideally he will be suspended so that just his toes brush the earth, allowing him a swinging freedom of movement à la Mad Max in the Thunderdome.

The way the game works is, the boy being swung about in the tree gets "basted," or beaten, with heavily knotted handkerchiefs. Often a rock would be knotted into the kerchief to give it some

SLING THE MONKEY.

oomph, though I doubt any real boy would object to saving time and just filling socks with smashed bricks. As the author says, "With players who don't mind a little buffeting this game becomes exceedingly lively: an active monkey is very difficult to approach with safety, and of course gives much more life to the game."

The good news is, the Monkey also gets a weapon, and he may do his best to strike the horde of boys beating him, with the added advantage of being airborne. Whoever he hits has to be the new Monkey. And the beatings continue.

Baste the Bear

This variation of the beating games, of which there are many, derives from a centuries-old sport in which a restrained wild bear was set upon by trained dogs in a bloody fight for survival.

In this game, a boy, "the Bear," must get down on his hands and knees in a circle in the dirt and be tied with a rope to his "Keeper." The other boys proceed as they did with the swinging monkey; that is, they try to beat the child on the ground without being hit by the Keeper, who is protecting his charge but not allowed to let go of the Bear's rope or step outside the circle. The bear himself is given no weapon, but he is allowed to grab at the legs of any boy who dares come close, and though biting is not explicitly encouraged...it's not called "Bait the Toothless Granny," is it? The reverend warns against the temptation to soften the game for the Bear:

"In some places the bears stipulate for an extra coat or similar protection from their assailants, but that is an effeminacy to which no encouragement should be given."

BASTE THE BEAR

Q: I want to know more about lawn tennis and croquet. It seems far preferable to this violent blood-fest.

A: No. Men only played those "gender-inclusive" games for social and courtship reasons, because there were so few options to see ladies bend over or break a nonfatal sweat. *These* are the games truly meant for healthy young boys. "Violent" is a word used by fretful women who make their sons sit down to pee. There was absolutely no advantage in raising a boy to be gentle in the nineteenth century. He was not born into a gentle world, no matter his wealth or standing. Even the loftiest priest or prince would be loved and respected more if he could hold his own amid violence and terror. These games reminded a boy, ever so subconsciously, that pain was inevitable, whether it came in the form of disease, war, or hankies loaded with broken glass in the name of good times!

Q: Let's move on to toys. What are my options? And what are my child's average survival rates should she use them?

A: I'm sensing a decline in your morale. Fight it, darling. Show the fortitude your child deserves in a mother. Now, most children had blocks, a slate to draw on, and sundry simple homemade toys, from rag dolls to fishing poles. For babies, mothers could choose from a wide variety of choking hazards. In the eighth edition of *The Mother's Book,* first published in 1831, Lydia Maria Child

Nursery toys of a wealthy family, circa 1900.

tells us that the best thing for teething is "a large ivory ring, or a dollar worn smooth" for them to gnaw on. Also fun for babies is "a string of very large wooden beads, or shining buttons...no buttons but steel, wood, or ivory, are safe; if they have any portion of brass about them, they are injurious." And she reminds mothers never to use green string from which the color might be sucked off. "Painted toys are not wholesome at this age, when children are so prone to convey everything to the mouth."

Q: I'm not giving my babies buttons and coins to suck, no matter what color the string. But incidentally, why was green especially bad?

A: Oh. You know. Arsenic. It's really a marvelous chemical and ever so versatile. Which makes it so frustrating that humans keep expiring when overexposed to it. It was arsenic that gave the green dye of that era its richness of color. They used it in everything from fake flower petals to wallpaper. Historians think the prevalence of it in domestic objects, especially bedroom wallpaper, which would be commonly touched and constantly inhaled, accounts for some of the mystery illnesses Victorians suffered. They didn't have a problem with arsenic green in general. Just…babies best not swallow a lot of it.

Q: Agreed. But what about educational toys? The Victorian age paralleled the Industrial Revolution, so it was packed with developments in science, technology, engineering, and math. I'd like to introduce STEM toys as soon as possible. Particularly to my daughters.

A: Of course! Well, the interesting thing is, the way nineteenth-century life was lived, a young man was exposed to basic STEM principles constantly. All but the poshest of boys

Clarence and Alonzo behind the Wright Cycle Company. Picture by Orville and Wilbur Wright. Some kids had better STEM teachers than others.

would be helping with repairs around the home and family business, learning everything from well excavation to wheelwrighting, just as a matter of keeping the household running. Toys were often made by the child himself, using college-level geometry and engineering, whether it be kites or toy boats. And keeping your first gun clean and functioning would teach a boy a great deal about science.

Q: If I'm not giving my child buttons, I'm not giving him guns. Seriously, don't joke about kids and guns.

A: I'm not. And neither were they.

In 1891 our old friend Reverend Wood files "shooting" as a boy's sport between "sea-fishing" and a chapter containing instructions for using dandelion extract to fight liver complaints in your pet dog. He allows that a boy's first shotgun should be a single barrel, which, really, by 1891 was mostly manufactured for children anyway. He emphasized (as did every other piece of literature on the subject) that the most important thing about guns was not marksmanship but learning care and respect of the instrument. According to Wood, the best way to match a boy to a properly sized gun for his growing frame was to "take up several guns in succession in the maker's shop, and rapidly bringing them to the shoulder, aim them at the eye of the attendant, who will at once see when the aim is correct."

Q: Just...just...no.

A: I know. But remember, it's impossible for us to see guns the way the parents of the 1800s saw them. Guns provided food, and protection from very real threats in an untamed world. Guns prepared a boy for the constant cavalcade of war and conquest most Western nations were embroiled in throughout the century.

Sure, accidents happened and horrible choices were made, even

Because when the birds come to reclaim their feathers from your hat, you must be ready.

back then. That's why, except in cases of unfortunate sporting goods clerks, safety and training were indispensable. An anonymous letter to the editor of an 1890 edition of *Forest and Stream* titled "Shall the Boy Have a Gun?" explained how mastering a gun kept children from more dangerous pursuits and set them on the path to power.

> *Boys will have amusements. They ordinarily prefer amusements of a robust character. Their disposition for such sports ought to be cultivated. Such a hobby will attract them from vicious pastimes: such sports will develop their physical and mental powers. To deprive them of vigorous amusement is to dwarf their energies, to make them simply "hewers of wood and drawers of water"—underlings.*

If it's any consolation, lawmakers were trying to differentiate between the weapon and the toy.

Toward the end of the nineteenth century at least one state, Indiana, passed a law saying that children's cap guns couldn't contain the same chemicals that real guns used, or at least not in the same amounts. You could get yourself a ten-dollar fine for that sort of shenanigan.

Q: Did they at least teach girls the mechanics of firearms and geometry of kite-making and…so forth? (I cannot believe I'm asking this.)

A: I'm certain many parents did. But girls had other areas of interest to tend to.

Q: Of course. Pretending to be good little mothers and housewives.

A: Smile when you say that, my feminist friend. Smile, because in the Victorian era, training a little girl to accomplish the work of wife and mother wasn't much different from training her to bend the laws of Nature and Physics to her will.

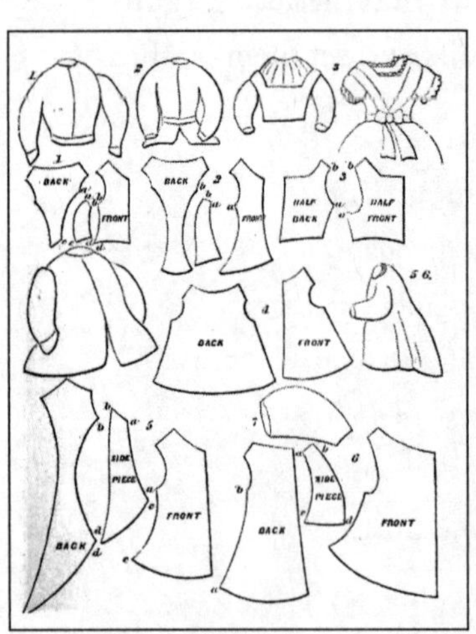

True, Victorians did not advocate gender equality past the age where both genders got to wear pretty dresses and have bouncy curls. But please don't think this means girls were excused from science and technology. Rather, they were trained in particular disciplines of it.

This is a pattern for a small girl to use to make doll clothes. She will of course have to measure the doll and re-size the pattern accordingly herself, requiring more applications of arithmetic than I care to consider.

And can you tell me how to build and sustain the perfectly tempered fire inside an iron oven? How much yeast will make your bread rise, depending on proportion of flour and surface area? For that matter, what sort of soil and how much moisture is required to grow the wheat that makes that flour? Hark...do I hear the call of science?

A growing girl was "STEMming" all over the place. Applied, real-life useful science and math.

Q: What about the sort of play that was not simply disguised labor? Did the girls get to beat each other with hankies and dangle from ropes too?

A: So now it's "get to"? You are just so touchy about gender.

Q: Well, I'm being sarcastic! I think. I...This century is just so confusing.

A: Well, I'm proud you're trying to untangle it. And of course girls didn't play those kinds of violent games. Have you already forgotten Romping Polly and her hilariously severed limb?

Playing outside and getting plenty of fresh air were fully supported in the nineteenth century, for girl and boy children alike. Just as long as they didn't play *together* or engage in the same activities. In fact, vigorous exercise in general was best done in private.

Take it from Lydia Maria Child, author of the popular 1856 book *The Moral, Intellectual, and Physical Training of the Young Explained:* "When I say that skating and sliding [sledding] are proper amusements for girls, I do not, of course, mean that they should mix in a public crowd. Such sports, when girls unite in them, should be confined to the inmates of the house, and away from all possibility of contact with the rude and vicious."

Q: So what sorts of things did girls do outside, properly and in public, that didn't result in dismemberment?

A: There were all sorts of approved public girl games! At least… variations on one game. According to *The Girls' Home Book, or How to Play and How to Work,* written in 1877 by Laura Valentine, recommended open-air activities included…holding hands in a circle. And singing a little.

That's…about it.

These made up a class of games among Victorian girls and today's three-year-olds called "Rounds." Sometimes clever girls could incorporate practice for future housework, as in Mrs. Valentine's version of "Here We Go Round the Mulberry Bush"!

The children all take hands and dance around, singing. Then they stop and pretend to wash their dresses, singing,

THE MULBERRY BUSH.

This is the way we wash our clothes,
Wash our clothes, wash our clothes!
This is the way we wash our clothes,
So early in the morning!

They then go on to wring out their clothes, then iron them. Or there is the "Swiss peasant" version where the girl gets to practice the motions of threshing wheat, sifting wheat, and resting on the ground after threshing and sifting wheat. So *that's* fun.

A particular favorite was "The Old Game of Honey-Pots." Bonus: This one is fun for the whole family, as older brothers and "Papa and Mama" are encouraged to participate, acting as "honey merchants and purchasers."

In this game, each girl represents an imported pot of honey, and the goal is to swing her in the arms of the stronger players. She holds her knees up and clasps her hands under them, and the number of swings she can endure before losing her grasp determines the value of her honey. But you can't just swing a girl. That'd be weird. There is a ceremony to it. Let us quote directly from Mrs. Valentine's game plan:

The purchaser approaches the merchant, and asks, Have you any good honey for sale, friend?

Honey Merchant. Yes, ma'am (or sir), first-rate. This pot is from Mount Hybla, the finest honey in the world; tastes of thyme, I assure you. This one is from Sicily, quite as good as any you would get at Fortnum and Mason's. Taste and try before you buy.

The purchaser then goes round, and pretends to taste the honey-pot. [I can't imagine this involves licking the children, which is the first method that comes to mind. Perhaps chewing a braid or nibbling a finger?]

THE OLD GAME OF HONEY-POTS.

Purchaser (shaking his head). Not very good. I see that everything Greek is best ancient. Ah! I like this Sicilian jar. How much will you sell it for?

Honey Merchant. A shilling a pound.

Purchaser. What does the jar weigh?

Honey Merchant. We will see, sir, if you will be good enough to help me.

And then they swing her. Fat little honey-pots are certainly the cheapest, and probably domestic.

Q: Do you really have to do all that talking?

A: First of all, females love pointless chatter, and bless this game for incorporating that natural feminine pleasure. Second, if you have a better way to teach a future housewife about the different quality variations of imported honey, I'd like to hear it.

Q: I want to say these games are sexist, but I'm not sure which gender they're sexist *against*.

A: Remember, our current Western lifestyle is a historical aberration. Most of us go our whole lives, no matter our gender, without having to rely on violence or physical strength to survive. Nineteenth-century boys held out no such hope. They were prepared from the earliest age for a life of battles, small and grand. Girls were trained to inspire love, create valued children, and keep warm a hearth, all done so well that a man is willing to risk his life to keep them safe. So, regarding girls' games, the more content you were with the prospect of doing laundry and letting someone gyrate you back and forth in the name of pleasure and health, the better off you would have been.

Q: Gross. Fine. Let's move on. What sorts of things were available for my children to read during this era?

A: Reading in moderation was encouraged, of course, but you can't just imprint any old book into a youth's impressionable mind. In fact, *most* books, especially fiction, are trouble. The problem with even "good" fiction, says Lydia Maria Child, is that even as it tries to condemn sin, "vices the juvenile reader never heard of, are introduced, dressed up in alluring characters, which excite their admiration, their love, their deepest pity."

For example, she cites a popular novel called *Charlotte Temple,* in which a girl is tricked into prostitution and dies miserably. It is

Give a girl a story about a girl who goes to a dance, is abandoned by her parents, becomes a prostitute, catches plague from eating rats, and dies alone in the gutter, and all they will remember is that there was a lovely dance.

her belief that teen girls will read this novel and, while barely noticing the overarching moral of the story, be introduced to the vice that scuppers the heroine. Especially since they don't quite know what "prostitution" is. "Wait...I could be paid money for dating handsome men? What am I doing hanging around *this* dump?" and before you know it they'll be enthusiastically knocking on the nearest brothel door.

Thus, children learn that flawed humans are deserving of compassion, and that they themselves aren't so bad for the occasional moral misstep. This notion, of course, *is utterly wrong by Victorian standards.* Good and evil never blur.

But if you insist on exposing a child to fictions, at least make sure they've been properly cleansed. Instead of reading the original Shakespeare, whose writing was barely disguised pornography, Mrs. Child recommends a special edition called *The Family Shakespeare,* "in which impure sentences are entirely omitted."

Bowdlerized Shakespeare, 1863.

Q: Oh, what? There were sexy parts in Shakespeare? Well, I sure didn't catch them during my sophomore-year English class. What does *The Family Shakespeare* leave out?

A: The original edition was edited by Thomas Bowdler and his sister Henrietta, though there would be countless copycats by the end of the nineteenth century. Bowdler liked Shakespeare, he really did. He liked to read the Bard aloud to his family but found that he kept having to skip the "dirty" parts and change the endings of all the tragedies. (His name became a verb: "Bowdlerize," meaning to cut out the saucy parts.) He expurgated all the references to sex, prostitutes, suicide...stuff that really has no place in tragedy or drama anyway, and changed them to something family-friendly.

He changed every exclamation of "God!" to "Heavens!" He made it clear that Ophelia's death was "accidental drowning." And he changed Iago's famous declaration "Your daughter and the Moor are now making the beast with two backs" in *Othello* to a very snoozy but proper "Your daughter and the Moor are now together." Most likely playing yard tennis while chaperoned.

"And then Juliet popped up and yelled 'Surprise!' and Romeo was all, 'Ah, you totally GOT me!' and they laughed and shared a root beer."

Q: Probably most young kids would find Shakespeare pretty boring.

A: All the better! As Mrs. Child tells us, we must not feed the "necessity of fierce excitement in reading [because it] is a sort of intellectual intemperance; and, like bodily intoxication, it produces weakness and delirium."

Q: What about *real* children's stories, like "Cinderella" and such?

A: Yes, fairy tales are an excellent choice, if told correctly. The heroines are flawless, the villains punished in a manner more depraved than you'd find in the darkest corners of the internet. This helps children learn that there is no gray area between good and bad.

Q: The fairy tales I remember aren't depraved! They're sweet and fun.

A: You're reading the wrong ones, then. Or rather, I suspect, watching the wrong ones, as presented to you by Disney. If you read the versions bestowed upon Victorian children and their ancestors, you find much sharper ideas of justice and virtue. Let's look at some familiar Disney heroines as first set forth by Jacob Grimm in the 1860 edition of his book *Home Stories.*

Rapunzel

In Grimm's version of "Rapunzel," the problem started with female greed. While pregnant, Rapunzel's mother started craving this radish-thing called "rampions" that grew only in the witch's private garden. She made her husband scale the fence and steal the radishes constantly. The witch eventually caught them and agreed to spare the thieving couple in exchange for their first-born. Which they were completely okay with, handed her right over. The witch really wasn't too terrible to Rapunzel, though she did lock her in a tower and use her hair as a ladder, same as always. Grimm never explains why, but I'm sure she had her reasons. Lots of parents homeschool their kids. But then when Rapunzel had become a young woman of fourteen, a prince discovered her, and they started dating in secret. Everything was fine until one day when Rapunzel was letting the witch up her hair and she announced, "Gee, you are a *lot* heavier than my boyfriend when I haul *him* up here."

Witch-Mother chopped off her hair, threw her into a desert wilderness, then used the hair to trick the prince into the tower. Upon hearing that Rapunzel was lost, he tried to commit suicide but instead just landed eyeballs-first in briars, becoming blind.

And…then he wandered a few years, eating berries and nuts. Eventually he found Rapunzel and the twins he'd impregnated her with in the wilderness. And they lived as happily ever after as can be expected.

Q: In women's studies class I learned that the tower is a phallic symbol and Rapunzel's hair is actually her bisexual nature and the witch cut it off as a represent—

A: Hey! Neat! But we want to be careful with overanalysis. Four-year-olds can be real slouches when it comes to applying queer theory or Jung to literature. So we'll read these stories through their little eyes. And see if it doesn't send us careening back to the path of mild-natured obedience.

Snow White

Grimm's "Snow White" is pretty close to most other versions, even Disney's. Though Disney glosses over how ever-loving *dumb* that girl was. Sure, she was also only seven when her stepmother began to hate her because of her superior beauty, and she was still a child, though probably at least twelve, when she ran away to the dwarves.

But even for a twelve-year-old, Snow White was not the sharpest-cut diamond in the dwarf mine. Three times the stepmother came to see Snow White "in disguise"—each disguise being that of a tattered beggar lady. The first time she laced her bodice so tight that Snow White passed out but survived. So the stepmother came back a second time and gave her a poisoned comb, which made her pass out, but, again, she survived. Finally the apple. Snow White, who had wised up to the fact that every old lady who came to her door kept trying to kill her, wouldn't eat it unless the queen split it with her. The apple had two very distinct sides, one regular and one beautiful and rosy. Guess which side was poisoned?

Q: You know, "Fool me once, shame on you...fool me three times without altering your method in any notable way...and maybe I actually kind of deserve to die from a magic apple."

A: Be nice. She's just a kid, after all. And it just so happens that after biting the poisoned apple she was only *mostly* dead (I said that in Miracle Max's voice—did you hear it?). Dead enough to make the queen's mirror happy, but still so lifelike that the dwarves put her in a glass coffin. Just for pretty. The prince came and begged for the beautiful dead girl and was given her.

Q: Why did he want a dead girl in a glass box?

A: I don't...He probably needed a coffee table. Anyway, the jostling of her coffin by the Prince's servants dislodged the apple chunk caught in her throat and she woke up, obliged to marry the not-creepy prince who was in the process of transporting her corpse to his home.

The only part Disney softened was having the dwarves beat the queen to death off-screen with pickaxes instead of going Grimm's punishment route, which was to make her wear molten lead slippers and dance till she died. Actually, that's a toss-up.

Cinderella

Interestingly, in Grimm's version of "Cinderella," her father never died—he just *could not be bothered.* He lived with his new wife and his very pretty (not ugly) stepdaughters in comfortable indifference to Cinderella, who had been kicked out of her bed and had to sleep in the kitchen-fire hearth, thus the name. Her mom did die, however, and Cinderella planted a twig on her grave that grew into a magic tree, and it was from her mother's corpse-tree that all the magic ball gowns and such fell, including the gold (not glass) slippers. The tree also contained magic animals, particularly doves. And the prince actually courted her for much longer than in most of these stories; they met two or three times before falling in love.

Q: Hey, did it ever strike you in the cartoon that Prince Charming was gay, and *that's* why his dad had to shove every single woman in the kingdom in his face and force him to pick one? Remember how he kept yawning as all these pretty women were presented to him?

A: No…you're doing it again. You can't judge even made-up history by today's standards. He was bored because he hadn't met his soulmate yet. If he were gay he wouldn't have fallen in love with Cinderella.

Q: I think they were just buds. Like he saw her shiny dress from across the room and was like "Wow, I have GOT to find out who designed that!" And then they got to talking and it turned out they both loved dance-cleaning and landscaping with magic birds and she was probably like, "Dude, you need a beard so your dad will leave you alone and I'm totally fine with that because at home I sleep in a fireplace," and so they agreed to—

A: Doesn't matter! You won't be needing to show your children

"Omg, girl! It fits you so fine! I love it! You, I mean! I love you!"

the Disney version. The prince isn't so visibly disinterested in the female sex in the Grimm version. He's still unable to recall Cinderella's face or know anything about her except her shoe size, of course, as in every version.

Q: (Way too focused on designer shoes to remember what his "true love" looked like, huh? No, not gay at all.)

A: *Shhh.* Please. Now, in the Grimm version, when the prince went door-to-door looking for a foot small enough to fit the mystery shoe, the stepmother made the first stepsister cut off her toes to fit it, and the prince was satisfied with this arrangement and set off with the stepsister. Honestly, these fairy tales call not so much for a suspension of disbelief in magic, but that humans can be so breathtakingly stupid. Luckily, the magic doves from the dead-mom tree flagged down the prince, pointed out that there was blood all over the golden slipper, and sent him back to look again for his bride. Which he did, this time carrying off the second stepsister, whose mother had sliced off her heel so the shoe would fit, whereupon the magic doves had to repeat their ministrations. "Go back to the house and find the only girl there whose feet aren't mutilated." The prince did, finally recognized Cinderella, and off they went to be married. The magic doves pecked out the eyes of the stepsisters.

Q: Ew. Much worse than the Disney version. That's disgusting.

A: Yes, it's a bit old-world gruesome. Now, the original tale of Sleeping Beauty, *that's* disgusting.

Sleeping Beauty

If you just compare Grimm's tale to Disney's, they're not too different. (Don't complicate things with the movie *Maleficent;* nothing is more intolerable in Victorian culture than humanizing the villain.) But if you trace Grimm's sources, you end up with a tale called "Sun, Moon, and Talia" written in 1634 by Gianbattista Basile. And here we descend into hell.

In this old version of "Sleeping Beauty," it was foretold that, yes, the princess would be hurt by a spinning wheel, and her father banished all spinning wheels from the kingdom. Still, Talia found one in her fifteenth year, and got some flax stuck under the fingernail. Which killed her in that fairy-tale manner in which beautiful women stop breathing but stay dewy fresh. One day a king, not a prince, lost his falcon somewhere around the tower in which Talia had been enshrined. He climbed up to retrieve the bird, found her instead, and in the words of the English translator "admired her beauty for a while."

Q: No. Oh, c'mon, no. Oh, no—don't say it.

A: And so, nine months later when still-sorta-dead Talia gave birth to twins…

Q: DAMMIT!

A:…one of the twins sucked the flax out from beneath Dead Mama's finger, and she woke! And she was happy, overjoyed to see

that she had...acquired some babies, whom she named Sun and Moon! The king found her now awake, and that was not a dealbreaker for him. In fact he liked her, and began spending time with his new family.

Q: What happened to fairy tales providing clear punishment to evil?

A: Well, this story has that! Not for the king, of course, because rap—...rapturously admiring the beauty of an unconscious teen girl under your dominion wasn't considered evil in seventeenth-century Italy. No, the evil was what the king's *wife* did when she realized he was cheating on her: ordering the twins to be brought to her personal chef so that she could slaughter and feed them to her husband in an elaborate meal as vengeance for his betrayal—

Q. Stop. I'm out.

A: Wait! Happy ending, though! The cook took pity on the twins and hid them and fed the king goats instead (which the text calls "kids," so THAT's funny).

Q: Not laughing.

A: And eventually when the king found out what his wife had tried to do he had her burned alive and married Talia, who became the new queen! And...oh, *and*...the cook who spared the children got promoted! Isn't that great? Huh? So all's well that ends well.

Q: My child now officially only has books from Pixar movies and Dr. Seuss.

A: I think Andy from *Toy Story*'s dad is probably dead, you know. Probably was a cop, which is why Andy is so attached to the law enforcers Buzz and Woody. So sad. Also *Green Eggs and Ham* supports caving to peer pressure and ingesting things that seem off to you. Like, get on my yacht and drop this groovy green acid and you'll see a goat or maybe a freak-cat that wants to break into your house and smash stuff with his two little gremlin buddies...

All in all, children don't need a lot of parental guidance when they play. They grow by finding obstacles to what they want, and overcoming them. If we soften the edges too much, we get a kid who can't take a bruise. If we make playtime crazy fun exciting with store-bought toys and constant parental attention, we get a kid who expects life to be nonstop thrills. And if we let them read completely sanitized children's stories, we get a kid who can't handle the injustices and unhappy endings real life dispenses. The Victorians knew that. We'd do well to apply that knowledge to our twenty-first-century broods.

9

How Many Leeches Should Be Applied to a Broken Bone and What Weapons Serve Me Best in the Valiant Struggle Against Rectal Worms?

On Maintaining General Health

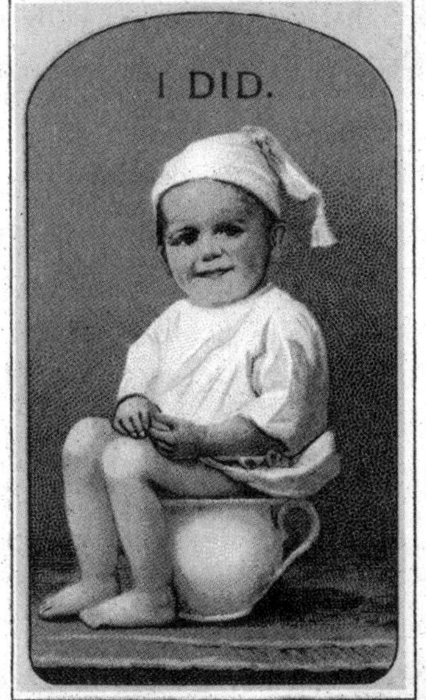

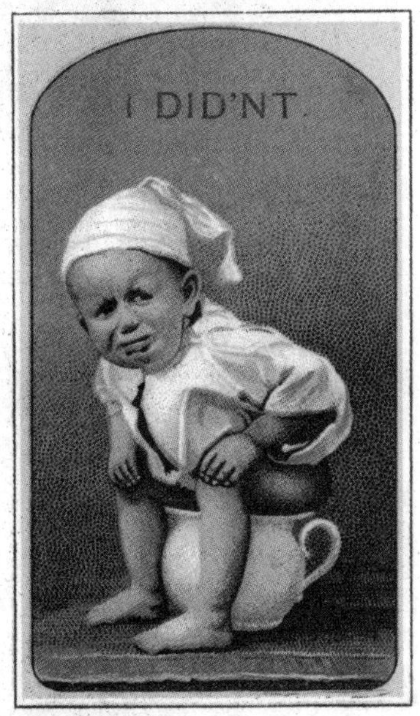

I have addressed the subject of children's health throughout this book, but since few other topics so seize the heart of a mother as the wellness of her child, I feel I owe you some further instruction. The majority of parenting books from the Victorian era focus on how to keep a child alive. I'm not going to do that. The twenty-first century, with its hygiene, safety practices, and medical science, will do the bulk of that work by itself, and may your gratitude for the time and place in which your child lives never cease.

But there's one area of medicine that Victorians knew how to do better than we do: Trial and error. By giving their children random plants and tinctures to see if anything happened, they often hit upon medications that, if not entirely effective or even safe, at least gave anxious parents something to do when their children fell ill. Which is a very powerful medicine indeed.

Here are some trusty staples to have in your medicine chest according to a person calling himself "a Physician of Philadelphia" in 1835's *The Home Book of Health.*

Q: Are these all going to be poisons?

A: You know, anything can be a poison if you use it incorrectly...But mostly, yes.

- **Strychnine (also called nux vomica)**—Nobody is saying this isn't one of the deadliest poisons known to man. So, use it carefully, all right? It's recommended for "cure of diseases of debility, for palsies, and amaurosis (sudden blindness). The commencing dose is half a grain of the extract in the evening, formed into a pill, and gradually increased to four or six grains."

A strychnine a day keeps the mortician at bay! Maybe!

- **Tin**—"Tin is sometimes used for the purpose of expelling worms from the intestines." Grind it into a powder, feed it to your child. It "disturbs the worms, and by its bulk and roughness carrying them before it." It might carry out some stuff they need, helpful bacteria or shreds of intestine and blood, too, so get ready for some complicated bowel movements.
- **Turpentine**—Four ounces a day will flush tapeworms right out. It's okay—turpentine is basically just toxic pine-tree juice. Also good for constipation, colic, and inflamed bowels, either in drink form or by enema. Topically you can use it on "indolent tumours and paralytic limbs," although the doctor doesn't specify anything curative will happen if you do.
- **Nitrate of silver**—Now, don't let the scary chemical name put you off. This concoction is known in the vernacular as "lunar caustic." Or "hell stone." Ah. None of those names sounds comforting. But that's okay—they sound something better. Effective!

To get lunar caustic, simply dissolve silver in nitric acid and harvest the powdered crystals when it dries. Easy peasy. You can use it, or at least the Victorians did, on anything you need to chemically scald off your body. And some of the things inside your body. Use it to remove "the callous edges of sores, strictures in the urethra, indolent ulcers and fistulous sores, and ringworm." Plus, it's an excellent dye for hair, ink, and, as your autopsy will later reveal, internal organs that are unfashionably pale.

Q: Wow. If silver can do all that, I imagine gold must be able to cure cancer, the common cold, and stank-butt combined.

A: Don't be ridiculous. There is no cure for stank-butt, and if there were it wouldn't be gold. Gold, according to the Physician of Philadelphia, at even one-fifteenth of a grain diluted into a neutral solvent, is a dangerous poison that will "excite severe and inflammatory symptoms." If your child is still suffering skin distresses after the application of silver nitrate, try drinking sarsaparilla.

Q: That sounds suspiciously pleasant!

A: But if the sarsaparilla causes the child to sweat, that's very bad and should "be checked by the addition of a little sulphuric acid."

Q: Ah…there we go. Hey, what's "castor"? I always read about kids having to take their castor oil.

A: Castor and castor *oil* are two entirely different medications, though both were used in the Victorian era. Castor is an oily fluid secreted from the anus pouches of the beaver. It was used for (not really at all) controlling epilepsy and in uterine complaints, until the price of beaver-butt oil became too expensive. Also, the smell was described as "nauseous." It is seldom used now.

"Oh, man! As if we weren't anxious enough when all they wanted was our pelts!"

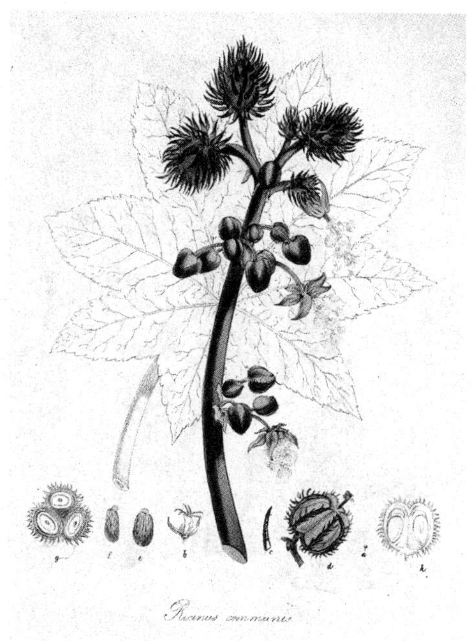

Deadly, disgusting, but oh, how it sluices clean your colon!

Q: Thank Go—

A: I'm sorry, "seldom used in medicine," I meant to say. It's a fairly popular food additive, helps round out the flavor of vanilla, especially. And as long as food companies use it in small enough amounts, they don't need to identify it as an ingredient on the package. It's usually listed as "natural flavoring."

Q: W…which foods? Which foods have the beaver-anus-pouch juice???

A: I have no idea. I avoid "natural ingredients." Never know what you're gonna get. Now, castor oil was and still is an extremely popular laxative. It has nothing to do with beaver bottoms, except the theory that sellers used the term "castor oil" to tell buyers that this product would do what the now-overpriced castor (desire for beaver pelts and anuses quickly outpaced supply) could do, but cheaper. The oil is pressed from the castor bean, *Ricinus communis.*

Q: Wait. Is that pronounced like "*rice*-inis"? Ricin, as in the lethal toxin? The most popular old-timey child's laxative comes from the same species of plant as *ricin*?

A: There's only one plant in the species, actually. So, yes, the deadly toxin and the medicine (still used today by itself and in the manufacture of other drugs) come from the same bean. It's a really complex bean.

"Madge, you get all that poison out of the castor bean before you squeezed the oil out? Well, never mind. Guess we'll find out!"

Q: This is what they gave to children? Who made it? Just some guy? What if they mishandled a batch? *Complex bean?*

A: You were so upset when you thought castor oil was made from anus squeezings, and now you're in a tizzy because it's derived from something as bland as a bean! Honestly, if you stay this fussy I'm not sure you're mother enough for Victorian health treatments.

Now, the reason the castor bean makes a good laxative is because its husk is indigestible to humans. In order to use it as a poison, you would need to crack it open, remove the bean meat, distill it into powder, and ingest it, whereupon, yes, you would die slowly and painfully. Or you'd have to chew the bean, which is very difficult, and not just one; it would take at *least* five beans to trigger an irreversible slide into death. More, if you have bad teeth!

Plus it tastes just terrible, which is why "castor oil" was used for punishments. It weeded out the truly sick children from those who were just trying to avoid their daily birching for whistling on school grounds. All in all, a handy substance to have in your pantry.

Although, if you listen to medical advice from earlier in the century, the best medicine is—

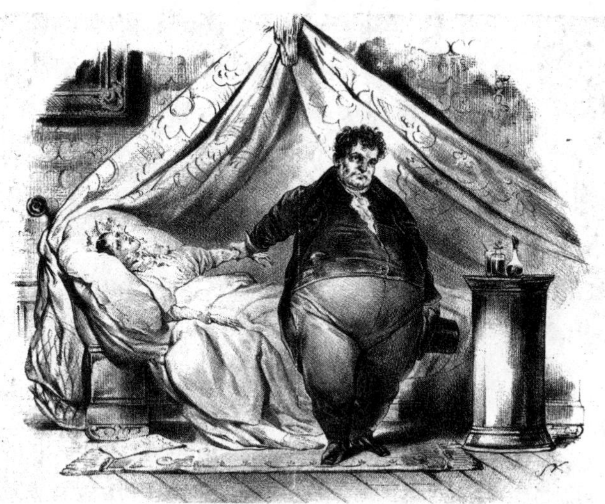

"Too much blood!" The obviously overblooded physician prepares to needlessly bleed the sallow patient.

Q: Laughter. Sleep. Fresh air. Love. Please, something not awful.

A:—bloodletting.

Q: Why would anyone ever assume a person has too much blood inside them?

A: Bleeding as medical practice was finally being phased out during the 1800s, after millennia of use to "balance the humors." During this time, the theory was that your health was controlled by your four most important organs—brain, lung, spleen, and gallbladder—and the fluids they secreted—blood, phlegm, black bile, yellow bile. If you were sick, physicians would determine which substance was crowding in on the others, and then try to drain some of it out of you. It wasn't always by bloodletting. Sometimes the doctor would give you something to cause vomiting, diarrhea, or more frequent, more yellow, urination.

By the early 1800s such ancient foolishness had been replaced

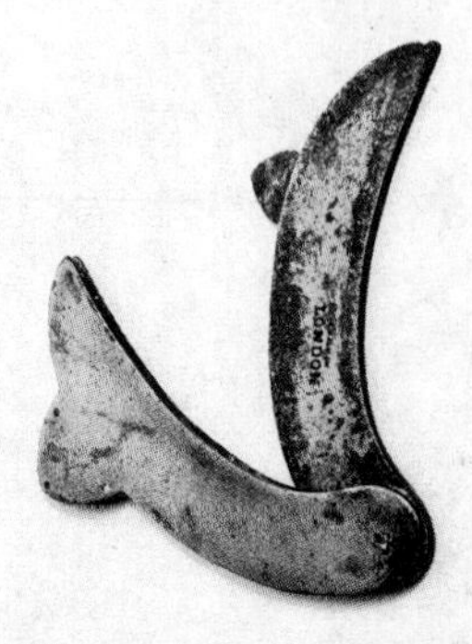

Bloodletting fleam. Like a can punch or bottle opener. But for people!

by harder science. Humors? What nonsense. Your illness was obviously being caused by a particular *organ* having too much blood in it. Indigestion? Try leeches on the tummy. Problem solved! High blood pressure? Well, you can't have high blood pressure if you've got no blood! If your patient turns a nice clean white color and passes out, you know you've drained away the problem.

Q: And how would I go about doing this horrible thing I'm not going to do?

A: Bloodletting for children wasn't as intense as it was for adults. It was not recommended that a standard fleam (a sharp metal device designed to directly puncture a vein) be used. By the nineteenth century people were starting to suspect that draining too much blood wasn't actually a cure. It just looked like one. Our "Physician of Philadelphia" explains that excessive bloodletting will just cause the patient to make even more blood to compensate, and we don't want that.

In fact, constant bleeding "proves only a palliative remedy, which sooner or later greatly enervates the body, deranges its functions, induces a premature old age, and calls for a more frequent resort to the operation."

Q: That's fine. I'm probably not going to...

A: Especially for children, it really was recommended you use something less invasive than ripping open a vein.

Q: Phew. I was gonna say...

A: So we're going to need leeches to get the job done.

Q:..."Where are the leeches?" is what I was going to say. Because we're in hell now and I assumed there would be leeches.

When not just any leech will do... Syme's Drug.

A: I will ignore your sarcasm and compliment the "can-do spirit" of the Victorian mother you're displaying. According to *The Home Book of Health,* "In children, where it is so difficult to get blood from a vein, leeches furnish an excellent resource." And what ailments do they treat? Just a partial list from the Philadelphia physician includes "various inflammatory diseases, as ophthalmia [inflammation of the eyes], sore throat, rheumatism, tooth-ache, inflammation of the bowels, and uterus; in measles and scarlet fever, in hooping-cough [*sic*], in head-ache, in bruises and in piles."

Q: So after all the time you've spent telling me my kid was going to get worms, now you say worms are good. Horrid, bloodsucking worms cure everything.

A: Except for conditions caused by other worms.

Q: How many worms cause "conditions"?

A: Oh gosh. *All* the worms, nearly. Tapeworms, roundworms, and, most commonly, pinworms. These are all different worms that are consumed by the child in egg form, attach to the digestive tract, grow large, and make life miserable. Which is another reason it's important to feed your child only boiled and flavorless

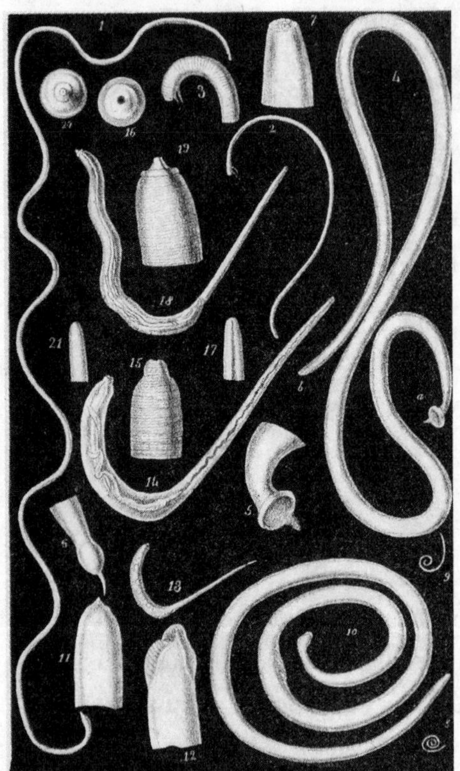

A few common intestinal worms that want to live in your child.

food. Undercooked and unrefrigerated meat, even when relatively fresh, carries worm eggs, as do fruits and vegetables not treated with pesticides. And even if you somehow manage to avoid all that, well, you can't change the fact that kids are grody little butt-pickers.

Q: My child is *not*—

A: Oh, stop. You know he is. And you were too. As Dr. Charles Townsend explains in an 1895 edition of *Babyhood: The Mother's Nursery Guide*, when the child "scratches with its fingers about the back passage and gets the eggs under its finger nails," he "easily passes them to its mouth and to its toys. In this way the eggs are swallowed by the child itself and by its companions who handle the toys. Food that is passed about by these children becomes a carrier of the infection."

So there you have it. The child scratches the itchy bits (and let us take a moment to solemnly dwell upon the fact that toilet paper is not yet in common usage), then touches toys and doorknobs, jams her fingers in a sister's mouth to reclaim a lost marble, and so forth. And the circle of vermin continues. Pinworms were the most common childhood infestation in the nineteenth century, not including lice, of course.

Q: How do I de-worm my child? (I hate you for making me ask that.)

A: (Then use modern pesticides on your garden, hippie.) First, you have to make sure the child actually has worms. Also called "thread worms" or "seat worms," pinworms are small white worms that set up shop in the rectum, where there are endless soft creases and folds for them to live and breed in. When the child relaxes in sleep, the worms will often scooch out for some fresh air through the rectum, where a vigilant mother should be waiting to catch them. Or be checking every poop a child proffers for signs of same.

Q: So...do I have to use the ricin oil, the beaver-butt squeezings, the booze, or the regular poisons for this one?

A: Pretty much any and all are acceptable. Just as long as you administer them in the form of a clyster.

Q: Clyster. And what fresh hell might that be?

A: Clysters, also referred to politely as "injections," were not exactly enemas. They *could* be, but they could also be so much more! *A Dictionary of Medicine, Designed for Popular Use* in 1854, defines a clyster as the process by which "substances are thrown into the rectum by mechanical means." Not placed, not inserted, mind you, but "thrown," *hurled* into that end zone as if by Brett Favre himself. In cases of worms, there were endless popular "vermicides," from garlic to turpentine. "Gaseous" clysters—including tobacco-smoke enemas—were also in

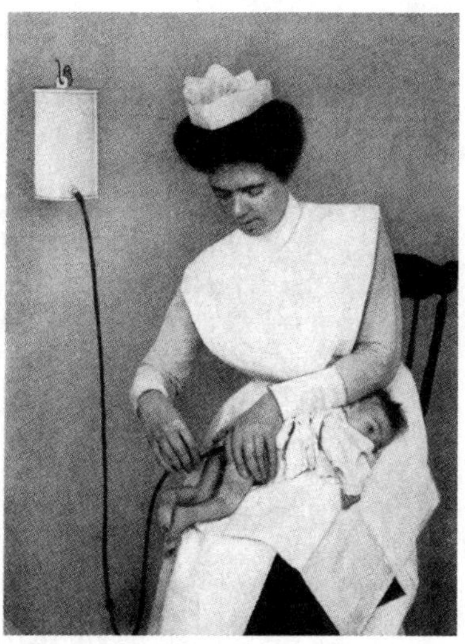

"Ma'am, please...I'm very tiny. Anything stronger than a drip and I'll be shot across the room!"

use until around midcentury, not only for worms but to relax constipation, induce labor, and control epilepsy.

Q: So, they literally blew smoke up people's ass—

A:—*ass*uredly stubborn cases of nervous and digestive ailments, yes. By the mid-1800s doctors were starting to realize that tobacco smoke really only seemed to do any good when inhaled. Though initially, as noted in the 1840 edition of Pereira's *The Elements of Materia Medica,* it was found to produce coughing fits in asthmatics.

Q: You don't say.

A: But press through that discomfort! Further testing showed that with continued use, inhaling tobacco had a calming effect on edgy patients.

Q:...

A: Before you go judging, remember, one day your great-grandchildren will be astounded at your stupidity for thinking deodorant actually made you less stinky when you could have just gotten your sweat glands surgically altered to perfume the air with chicory, which will likely be the preferred scent of the time.

Anyway, I haven't told you the greatest danger (according to Victorians) of pinworms. Those wandering little hands do more damage than you know. As Martin Lamont warns us in 1861's "Medical Adviser and Marriage Guide":

> *It is a deplorable fact, that young ladies, as well as youth of the opposite sex, are addicted to the habit of self-abuse to an alarming extent. This habit frequently has its origin in irritation of the genitals and lower bowels of children, from costiveness, or from pinworms...the frequent inclination to rub or scratch the*

> *adjacent parts lead to the practice of Self-Pollution.*

Plate 20—*Figure* 53.—Horrible appearance of the Features caused by Self-Abuse.

Q: Self-pollution? Like, masturbation? Worms all up in a poor kid's business and *that's* what they were worried about?

A: There was a large and widely published school of health reformers in the mid to late nineteenth century who thought masturbation, always begun in childhood, caused nearly every disease. Children were to be taught that "self-abuse" was a "vice which exhausts the body, destroys the eye-sight, impairs digestion and circulation, deranges the brain and nervous system in an astonishingly short time, thereby impairing the mind, destroys the possibility of a healthy offspring, and stamps the face with its marks and signs as visibly as does the small-pox." Licentiousness and prostitution had their root in this practice, of course, as well as death itself, according to Orson Squire Fowler, who announced, "Women…are dying by thousands, of consumption, of female complaints, of nervous or spinal affections, of general debility, and of other ostensible complaints innumerable, and some of insanity, caused by this practice."

Q: Okay, you know what? You're giving me a gaseous clyster right

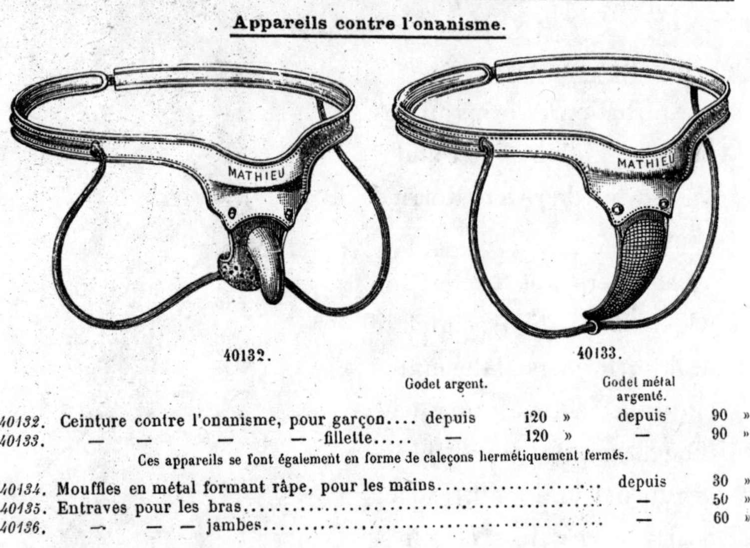

Maison MATHIEU. — Paris et Lyon. 411

Appareils contre l'onanisme.

		Godet argent.		Godet métal argenté.	
40132.	Ceinture contre l'onanisme, pour garçon....	depuis	120 »	depuis	90 »
40133.	— — — — fillette.....	—	120 »	—	90 »

Ces appareils se font également en forme de caleçons hermétiquement fermés.

40134.	Moufles en métal formant râpe, pour les mains....................	depuis	30 »
40135.	Entraves pour les bras..	—	50 »
40136.	— — — jambes..	—	60 »

Anti-masturbation apparatus for little boys and girls.

now with this nonsense. What foolishness! It's totally natural for a child to explore his or her body.

A: You keep thinking the Victorians regarded "natural" things as good. Remember, Original Sin pulses through the heart of even the most cuddlesome infant. Parents and physicians took great pains to stop a child's "natural" exploration of her body.

Q: How?

A: In horrible ways. Serrated rings that encircled the penis. Little girls fitted with steel plating between their legs to protect their genitalia from their own hands. Tying the hands of a child to a bedpost while they slept. And these were the nonsurgical interventions. It's the stuff of nightmares and I'd rather not dwell on it.

Thankfully, by 1901, when Emma Frances Angell Drake wrote

What a Young Wife Ought to Know, views on childhood masturbation seem to have progressed some, and there was less emphasis on shaming or physically restraining the child. In fact, Drake encouraged mothers to remember that even though the practice was evil, the practitioner was innocent. Says Drake, "Above all, do not treat your child, even if the habit is formed before you discover it, as if he were a criminal. He is unfortunate, and ignorant of the wrong or the danger he is in."

Q: Oh, those poor kids. Somehow this whole section makes me sadder than all the worm infestations and rat-poison medication combined.

A: I know. There's little comfort I can give you, except to remind you that this time passed. And in fact, some of the very children who were raised under the duress of sexual stigma would later be rouging their kneecaps and dancing the Charleston to speakeasy jazz! Until the Great Depression hit and the food went away. But then Hitler would really start up our economy again! All those men dead in war, though. Which made the survivors determined to live picture-perfect lives! Which stunted the emotional growth of the Baby Boomer generation. Which in turn gave us the freedom of the 1960s cultural revolution! Of course that led—

Q: Stop. I get it. Our society is a wheel. Misery and contentment will continue to trade places for eternity in a never-ending cycle.

A: . . . Uh . . . yeah. That's what I was going for. Totally.

Q: Just one last question. Why did the Victorians keep using dangerous medicines and subscribing to damaging theories that obviously didn't work for so long?

A: I will answer that if you can answer me this: How, in precise language, does swallowing two weeks' worth of pills labeled "penicillin" make your cough go away? Can you tell me, here and now, without Googling? And if you can, what about that time your great-aunt took penicillin and more, but was so ill, she passed anyway? Was her medication a sham, or the disease simply too powerful?

You see, the Victorians had no reason to believe their methods didn't "work."

Sometimes they *did* work, and patients fully recovered. We would consider that mere correlation, knowing what we know, but the Victorians saw causation. Sometimes the patient was simply too sick and died despite the treatment (or sometimes, as we now know, because of it).

We continue to use treatments that we don't understand today. I doubt you've read the published research on the trials of drugs before you use them. You aren't supposed to have to. You don't have the time or expertise to master the mysteries of the human body, so you rely on people who've devoted their lives to the subject to interpret the evidence for you. If your disease turns out to be treatable, you're rewarded for your faith. If not, the doctors will still do all they can, whether it be chemotherapy or, once upon a time, bloodletting and opiates.

10

The Successful Mother: Are You She?

Beth Balmer, age three.
The author attests: product and producer of superior mothers.

As we conclude our brief overview of raising the perfect child, you are no doubt anxious to see if these methods will yield you the child of your dreams. If, as illustrated by the popular "The Two Paths" drawings of the late nineteenth century, your child will grow into a beloved elder, or a destitute deviant. To figure this, we must—

Q: You stop right there, you twisted harpy. I bought this book in good faith. It says on the cover, "Guide to Raising Flawless Children," and instead of anything I can use, I find page after page of various tortures, poisons, and sexism to inflict on my child. This is not a child-rearing book. This is a guided tour of the nine circles of hell.

A: What were you expecting?

Q: I don't know! Secret recipes for sore throats! Little behavior modifiers left behind by time!

A: I provided those. Caustic silver nitrate, and fastidious birching. I presumed you had already tried the less invasive options and found them wanting.

Q: You know, even if I weed out the crazy, I don't think I could use hardly anything you've taught me in this book.

A: Why, do you suppose?

Q: Because my kids aren't Victorian! I can't pretend we live in a world where children are burdens or showpieces. I'm not just dealing with someone that's going to turn into a human. I'm dealing with a human the whole time.

A: Human the whole time? That's rather generous.

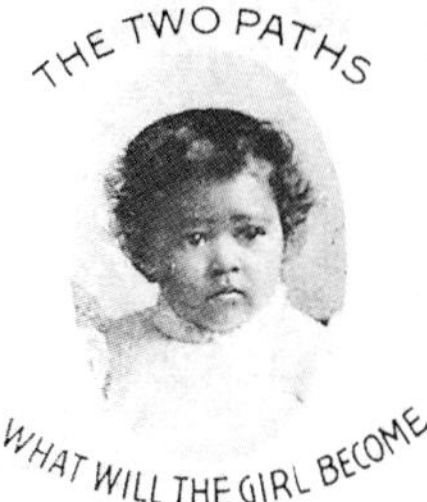

BAD LITERATURE

STUDY AND OBEDIENCE

FLIRTING AND COQUETTERY

VIRTUE AND DEVOTION

FAST LIFE DISSIPATION

A LOVING MOTHER

AN OUTCAST

Copyright, 1905, by J. A. Hertel.

AN HONORED GRANDMOTHER

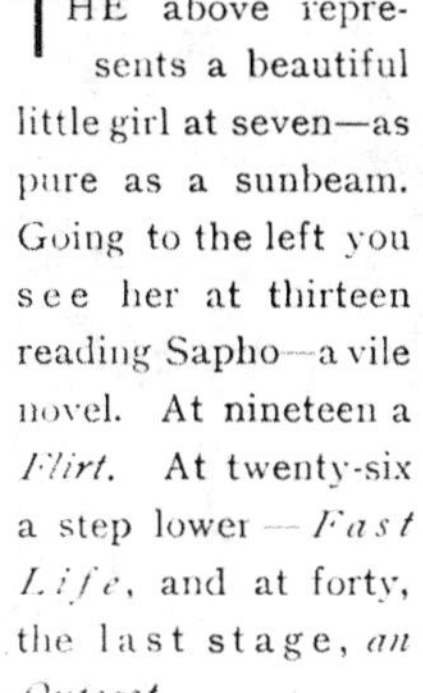

THE above represents a beautiful little girl at seven—as pure as a sunbeam. Going to the left you see her at thirteen reading Sapho—a vile novel. At nineteen a *Flirt*. At twenty-six a step lower—*Fast Life*, and at forty, the last stage, *an Outcast*.

To the right we have a brighter picture—*Study and Obedience, Virtue and Devotion*. Next, *motherhood*—Woman's greatest blessing. At sixty, an honored and beloved grandmother.

YOUTH.

MANHOOD.

MIDDLE LIFE.

AGE.

CHILDHOOD.

TWO PATHS IN LIFE.

THESE contrasted pictures furnish texts for a whole volume of sermons upon human life and destiny. The CHILD stands at the parting of the ways, and he may run through in succession all the phases depicted in either series of portraits. The essential elements of either course of development lie alike in those smooth features. Which shall be actually realized depends mainly upon the influences brought to bear upon him from without. A few years of training in our schools upon the one hand, or in the streets upon the other, will make all the difference, in the YOUTH, between the characters that stand opposed to each other in these opposite pictures. A youth of study and training in a few years moulds the lineaments of the face into the resemblance of the first picture of MANHOOD; while, by a law equally inevitable, idleness and dissipation bring out all the lower animal faculties, which reveal themselves in the depressed forehead, the hard eyebrow, the coarse mouth, and the thickened neck of the opposite picture. The short-boy, and rowdy, and blackleg, if he escapes the state prison and the gallows, passes, as he reaches the confines of MIDDLE AGE, into the drunken loafer, sneaking around the grog-shop in the chance of securing a *treat* from some one who knew him in his flush days; while he who has chosen the other path, as he passes the "mid journey of life," and slowly descends the slope toward AGE, grows daily richer in the love and esteem of those around him; and in the bosom of the family that gather about his hearth, lives over again his happy youth and earnest manhood. What a different picture is presented in the fate of him who has chosen the returnless downward path, another and almost the last stage of which is portrayed in the companion sketch of AGE. The shadows deepen as he descends the hill of life. He has been successively useless, a pest, and a burden to society, and when he dies there is not a soul to wish that his life had been prolonged. Two lives like these lie in possibility enfolded within every infant born into the world.

YOUTH.

MANHOOD.

MIDDLE LIFE.

AGE.

Q: I don't know. Even when they can't feed themselves and are pooping everywhere, it's not because they're bad and need to be punished and scolded like stubborn donkeys—

A: "Asses."

Q: Whatever—it's just that they're at that natural stage of development. And unlike the Victorians, I don't think "natural" is necessarily evil. I mean, I'd rather my kid crayoned every wall in the house than be smacked around by a schoolmaster for whispering to her friend. I'd rather pay a two-thousand-dollar ER bill because he accidentally ate poison than pay five dollars to have some quack purposely feed it to him. And I can't believe how much *shame* I was supposed to heap on them. Shame for being female, or not manly enough, for exploring their bodies, for asking the wrong questions. It's like the goal of Victorian child-rearing was to create a porcelain doll that would one day turn into a porcelain person. And it might have worked, in fact—it might have even been necessary for that time and place. I get that a smaller, harder world needs stricter rules.

But that's not my kid's world.

A: Huh. Interesting.

Q: Like that picture you put up there. There are *more* than two paths! My kids have so many different directions they can go in! Maybe choices were limited back then, but now there are so many. I'd rather teach them to govern themselves because they want a good life. And then make sure they're strong and self-sufficient enough to follow it through no matter how rough it gets. You didn't teach me much about that.

A: Well...I illustrated the pitfalls of reading, eating pickles, and angering the Old Testament God.

Q: You did, yes. Thank you.

A: So you mean to tell me you think this advice, though perhaps useful in a world and time far away from ours, is insufficient for today? And that, as you would with any parenting manual, you must carefully pick the pieces of advice that apply to your own life and child? That in fact, even though you might suffer during the process, you alone know how to raise *your* kid best?

Q: Don't pretend you planned that from the start.

A: Heaven forfend! Imagine writing a whole book with the goal of having the reader (who is far mouthier than she need be, might I add) reject the message! Insanity!

Q: I'm going to go make my kid empty the dishwasher to earn some screen time. She's been watching these weird YouTube clips that actually teach stuff.

A: Tolerance for cross-dressing puppets?

Q: Maybe. That'd be pretty cool. I'll watch it with her and find out.

The End

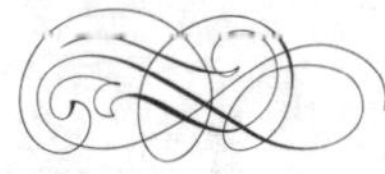

Bibliography

Abbott, John S. C. *The Mother at Home, or The Principles of Maternal Duty, Familiarly Illustrated.* New York: Harper and Brothers, 1855.

Aldrich, Virgil C. "A Theory of Ball-Play." *Psychological Review* 44 (1937): 395.

American Dental Association and William Morton. *Transactions of the American Dental Association.* American Dental Association, 1896.

Barker, Samuel. *The Domestic Management of Infants and Children in Health and Sickness.* London: Robert Hardwicke, 1875.

Barnett, Henrietta. *The Making of the Body: A Children's Book on Anatomy and Physiology.* London: Cassell, 1894.

Beck, John. *The Retrospect of Medicine.* New York: W. A. Townsend Publishing, 1863.

Benton, Caroline French. *The Mother's Book: A Handbook for the Physical, Mental and Moral Training of Children.* New York: University Society, 1919.

Black, Mary. *American Advertising Posters of the Nineteenth Century.* New York: Dover, 1976.

Bloomingdale Brothers. *Bloomingdale's Illustrated 1886 Catalog.* New York: Dover, 1997.

Blum, Stella. *Fashions and Costumes from Godey's Lady's Book.* New York: Dover, 1985.

——. *Victorian Fashions and Costumes from* Harper's Bazaar: *1867–1898.* New York: Dover, 1974.

Brochard, André Théodore. *The Young Mother's Guide on the Care and Education of the Infant.* London: Baillière, Tindall, and Cox, 1874.

Bull, Thomas. *The Maternal Management of Children, in Health and Disease.* New York: D. Appleton, 1849.

Carson, Gerald. *One for a Man, Two for a Horse: A Pictorial History, Grave and Comic, of Patent Medicines.* Garden City, NY: Doubleday, 1961.

Chapin, Henry Dwight. *Diseases of Infants and Children.* 1909. Reprinted, Sligo: HardPress, 2013.

Chavasse, Pye Henry, and Charles C. H. Chavasse. *Advice to a Mother on the Management of Her Children, and on the Treatment of Their Most Common Illnesses & Accidents.* London: Cassell, 1948.

Chicago (Ill.) Post-Graduate Medical School. *The North American Practitioner.* Vol. 2. Chicago: J. H. White, 1890.

Child, Lydia Maria. *Flowers for Children.* New York: C. S. Francis, 1856.

——. *The Mother's Book.* Glasgow: Richard Griffin, 1832.

Culbertson, J. C., and L. C. Windsor. "The Obstetric Gazette." *Obstetric Gazette* 10 (Jan. 1887): 278.

Dalton, Rose. "Disciplining Children." *Good Housekeeping,* 1886.

Drake, Emma Frances Angell. *What a Young Wife Ought to Know.* Philadelphia: Vir, 1901.

Dwight, Theodore. *The Father's Book, or Suggestions for the Government and Instruction of Young Children, on Principles Appropriate to a Christian Country,* 2nd ed. Springfield, MA: G. and C. Merriam, 1835.

Dye, John H. *Illustrated Edition of Painless Childbirth, or Healthy Mothers and Healthy Children: A Book for All Women.* Buffalo, NY: Dr. J. H. Dye Medical Institute, 1912.

Ellis, Havelock. *Studies in the Psychology of Sex.* Philadelphia: F. A. Davis, 1928.

——— et al. *Sexual Inversion: A Critical Edition.* 1897. Reprinted, London: Palgrave Macmillan, 2008.

Engelmann, George Julius. *The American Girl of To-day: The Influence of Modern Education on Functional Development.* Boston, 1901.

———. *Labor Among Primitive Peoples.* St. Louis, MO: J. H. Chambers, 1883.

Epps, John. *Constipation: Its Theory and Cure.* London: Piper, Stephenson, and Spence, 1854.

Evans, Herbert M., and Miriam E. Simpson. "Aschheim-Zondek Test for Pregnancy." *California and Western Medicine* 32 (March 1930): 145–48.

Fass, Paula S. *Childhood in America.* New York: New York University Press, 2000.

Foote, Edward B. *Plain Home Talk.* New York: Murray Hill, 1889.

Fowler, O. S. *Self-Culture, and Perfection of Character, Including the Management of Youth.* New York: Fowler, 1894.

Galabin, Alfred Lewis. *A Manual of Midwifery.* London: J. and A. Churchill, 1904.

Giudice, Marco Del. "The Twentieth Century Reversal of Pink-Blue Gender Coding: A Scientific Urban Legend?" *Archives of Sexual Behavior* 41, no. 6 (2012): 1321–23.

Grafton, John. *New York in the Nineteenth Century: 317 Engravings from* Harper's Weekly *and Other Contemporary Sources.* New York: Dover, 1980.

Greenstone, Gerry, M.D. "The History of Bloodletting." *BC Medical Journal* 52, no. 1 (Jan.–Feb. 2010): 12–14. www.bcmj.org/premise/history-bloodletting

Gregory, John. *A Father's Legacy to His Daughters.* Printed for W. Strahan, T. Cadell in the Strand, and J. Balfour and W. Creech at Edinburgh, 1774.

Guerber, H. A. *Yourself and Your House Wonderful.* Philadelphia: Uplift, 1913.

Hand-Book of Nursing for Family and General Use, A. Philadelphia: J. B. Lippincott, 1901.

Hoffmann, Heinrich. *Der Struwwelpeter.* 1845. Reprinted, New York: Dover, 1995.

———. *Slovenly Betsy.* 1911. Reprinted, Carlisle, MA: Applewood Books, 1995.

Holmes, Oliver Wendell. "Contagiousness of Puerperal Fever." *New England Quarterly Journal of Medicine,* 1843.

Horner, William E. *The Family Doctor, or The Home Book of Health and Medicine: A Popular Treatise on the Means of Avoiding and Curing Diseases and of Preserving the Health and Vigour of the Body to the Latest Period, Including an Account of the Nature and Properties of Remedies, the Treatment of the Diseases of Women and Children, and the Management of Pregnancy and Parturition.* New York: Saxton, Barker, 1859.

Imray, Keith. *A Popular Cyclopedia of Modern Domestic Medicine: Comprising Every Recent Improvement in Medical Knowledge.* New York: Collins, 1866.

Jacobi, Mary Putnam. *The Question of Rest for Women During Menstruation.* New York: G. P. Putnam's Sons, 1877.

Jefferis, B. G., and J. L. Nichols. *Searchlights on Health: The Science of Eugenics; a Guide to Purity and Physical Manhood, Advice to Maiden,*

Wife and Mother, Love, Courtship, and Marriage. Naperville, IL: J. L. Nichols, 1919.

Kings of Israel and Judah: Their History Explained to Children, Being a Continuation of "Lines Left Out," by the Author of "Peep of Day" &c. London: Hatchards, Piccadilly, 1872. ufdc.ufl.edu/UF00026237/00001/462j?search=rehoboam.

Macaulay, Alexander. *A Dictionary of Medicine, Designed for Popular Use.* Edinburgh: Adam and Charles Black, 1849.

MacDonald, James Joseph, and Julian Alvin Carroll Chandler, eds. *Life in Old Virginia: A Description of Virginia More Particularly the Tidewater Section, Narrating Many Incidents Relating to the Manners and Customs of Old Virginia So Fast Disappearing as a Result of the War Between the States, Together with Many Humorous Stories.* Norfolk: Old Virginia, 1907.

McCormick, John Henry. *Century Book of Health: The Maintenance of Health; Prevention and Care of Disease; Motherhood; Care, Feeding and Diseases of Children; Modern Home Nursing; Accidents and Emergencies; Injurious Habits; a Complete Practical Guide.* Springfield, MA: King-Richardson, 1907.

Melendy, Mary Ries. *The Ideal Woman: For Maidens, Wives, Mothers; a Book Giving Full Information on All the Mysterious and Complex Matters Pertaining to Women; Creative Science; Bearing, Nursing and Rearing Children; Hints on Courtship and Marriage; Limitation of Offspring; Health, Mental and Physical Beauty, Etc. Etc.; Including Diseases Peculiar to Women, Their Treatment and Cure.* Wm. Gribble, 1913.

Moll, Albert. *The Sexual Life of the Child.* New York: Macmillan, 1923.

Moncrieff, A. R. Hope. *A Book About Boys.* 1886. Reprinted, Sydney: Wentworth Press, 2016.

Montgomery Ward. Montgomery Ward & Co. 1894–95 Catalogue & Buyers Guide, no. 56. Chicago: Follett, 1970.

Morten, Honnor. *Humane Review,* 1900.

Morton, William J., and Walter Brickner. *International Journal of Medicine and Surgery* 17 (1903).

Mother [pseud.]. *A Few Suggestions to Mothers on the Management of Their Children.* London: J. and A. Churchill, 1884.

Mulierology, or The Science of Woman: A Guide to Health, Beauty, and Happiness for the Maiden, Wife and Mother, Profusely Illustrated. W. H. Ives, 1889.

Napheys, George H. *The Physical Life of Woman: Advice to the Maiden, Wife, and Mother.* London: Homœopathic, 1895.

Partridge, Eric. *A Dictionary of Slang and Unconventional English; Colloquialisms and Catch Phrases, Fossilised Jokes and Puns, General Nicknames, Vulgarisms and Such Americanisms as Have Been Naturalised.* London: Routledge, 2002.

Perry, Claire. *Young America: Childhood in Nineteenth-Century Art and Culture.* New Haven, CT: Yale University Press, 2006.

Perry, George, and Nicholas Mason. *The Victorians: A World Built to Last.* New York: Viking, 1974.

Pryor, William. *The American Gynaecological and Obstetrical Journal: Formerly the New York Journal of Gynaecology and Obstetrics.* Vol. 3. Ann Arbor: University of Michigan, 1894.

Pullman, Philip. *Fairy Tales from the Brothers Grimm: A New English Version.* New York: Viking Penguin, 2012.

Rice, Nathan P. *Trials of a Public Benefactor, as Illustrated in the Discovery of Etherization.* New York: Pudney and Russell, 1859.

Riddell, Newton N. *Child Culture According to the Laws of Physiological Psychology and Mental Suggestion.* Chicago: Child of Light Publishing, 1902.

Riis, Jacob A. *The Children of the Poor.* New York: C. Scribner's Sons, 1892.

Robinson, Charles H., ed. *The Science of Eugenics and Sex Life: The Regeneration of the Human Race*. W. R. Vansant, 1904.

Rohe, George H. *Text-Book of Hygiene: A Comprehensive Treatise on the Principles and Practice of Preventive...Medicine from an American Standpoint. American Journal of Public Health*, 1912.

Roscoe, Henry. *Roscoe's Digest of the Law of Evidence in Criminal Cases.* Vol. 2. Philadelphia: T. and J. W. Johnson, 1888.

Routledge, Edmund. *Every Boy's Annual.* London: Routledge, Warne and Routledge, 1869.

Rushton, Alan R. *Royal Maladies: Inherited Diseases in the Ruling Houses of Europe.* Victoria, BC: Trafford Publishing, 2008.

Ryan, Michael. *Manual of Medical Jurisprudence.* London: Renshaw and Rush, 1831.

Sansom, William. *Victorian Life in Photographs.* London: Thames and Hudson, 1974.

Schorsch, Anita. *Images of Childhood: An Illustrated Social History.* New York: Mayflower Books, 1979.

Schroeder, Karl. *A Manual of Midwifery.* New York: D. Appleton, 1873.

Shannon, Thomas Washington. *Nature's Secrets Revealed: Scientific Knowledge of the Laws of Sex Life and Heredity, or Eugenics: Vital Information for the Married and Marriageable of All Ages... Together with Important Hints on Social Purity, Heredity, Physical Manhood and Womanhood by Noted Specialists, Embracing a Department on Ethics of the Unmarried.* 1904. Reprinted, Garden City, NY: Doubleday, 1970.

Shew, Joel. *The Water-Cure in Pregnancy and Childbirth: Illustrated with Cases Showing the Remarkable Effects of Water in Mitigating the Pains and Perils of the Parturient State.* New York: Fowler and Wells, 1849.

Shrady, George Frederick, and Thomas Lathrop Stedman. *Medical Record.* Vol. 26. W. Wood, 1884.

Sigourney, L. H. *Letters to Mothers.* Hartford, CT: Hudson and Skinner, 1838.

Smith, Elmer Lewis. *Patent Medicine: The Golden Days of Quackery.* Lebanon, PA: Applied Arts Publishers, 1973.

Souden, David. *Victorian Village.* London: Collins and Brown, 1991.

Sperry, Lyman Beecher. *Husband and Wife: A Book of Information and Advice for the Married and the Marriageable.* Grand Rapids, MI: F. H. Revell, 1900.

Stefferud, D. "Germany Gets Tighter Rule by Dictator." *Evening Independent,* June 27, 1935.

Stella, Jacques. *Games and Pastimes of Childhood.* 1657. Reprinted, New York: Dover, 1969.

Stevens, John. *Man-Midwifery Exposed, or The Danger and Immorality of Employing Men in Midwifery Proved; and the Remedy for the Evil Found.* London: Caudwell, 1866.

Tayler, Charles B. *May You Like It, by a Country Curate.* T. Boys, 1822.

Taylor, Alfred Swaine, and Edward Hartshorne. *Medical Jurisprudence.* 1853. Reprinted, Holmes Beach, FL: Gaunt, 2011.

Thorburn, John. *Female Education from a Physiological Point of View: A Lecture…* Manchester: J. E. Cornish, 1884.

Toye, Edwin J. Letter. *Lancet.* 1901.

Tuthill, Louisa Caroline. *The Nursery Book for Young Mothers.* New York: G. P. Putnam, 1849.

Valentine, L. *The Girls' Home Book, or How to Play and How to Work.* London: F. Warne, 1877.

Victoria. *Letters of Queen Victoria: A Selection from Her Majesty's Correspondence Between the Years 1837 and 1861.* 1908. Reprinted, London: Forgotten Books, 2016.

Weaver, G. S. *Hopes and Helps for the Young of Both Sexes: Relating to the Formation of Character, Choice of Avocation, Health, Amusement, Music, Conversation, Cultivation of Intellect, Moral Sentiment, Social Affection, Courtship, and Marriage.* New York: Fowler and Wells, 1887.

Wesley, John. "The Doctrine of Original Sin." In *The Doctrine of Original Sin: Extracted from a Late Author* by Thomas Boston. London, 1785.

West, John D. *Maidenhood and Motherhood, or Ten Phases of a Woman's Life: How to Protect the Health, Contribute to the Physical and Mental Development, and Increase the Happiness of Womankind.* Chicago: Wabash Publishing House, 1886.

Willard, Emma. *Plan for Improving Female Education.* Middlebury, VT: J. W. Copeland, 1819.

Wilson, M. A. *American Science and Invention: A Pictorial History.* New York: Simon and Schuster, 1954.

Wood, John George. *The Boy's Modern Playmate: A Book of Sports, Games, and Pastimes.* London: Frederick Warne, 1891.

Yale, Leroy M. "General Interests of the Nursery." *Babyhood: The Mother's Nursery Guide,* November 1895.

Yandell, D. W. et al. *The American Practitioner.* Vols. 21–22. Louisville, KY: John P. Morton, 1896.

Youman, A. E., and Katie F. Hamilton. *A Dictionary of Everyday Wants.* New York: F. M. Reed, 1872.